Fashion Diva

My Life, Loves, and Lessons

Fashion Diva

My Life, Loves, and Lessons

A Memoir by

Ollie McNamara

Silver Threads
San Diego, California

Fashion Diva: My Life, Loves, and Lessons: A Memoir

Silver Threads is an imprint of Silvercat™.

For information, contact:

Silver Threads
3930 Valley Centre Drive, PMB 102
San Diego, CA 92130
868-794-1597
www.silver-threads.org

ISBN 13: 978-1-893067-08-0
Library of Contress Control Number: 2007937387

printed in the United States of America

to

Cindy and James

Contents

ONE

Katarzyna and Wasyl

My Ukrainian Parents

Nothing could have prepared me for that tragic phone call.

It came on a dismal, grey, November afternoon in New York City while I worked in my office on the seventh floor at Saks Fifth Avenue. Hours of wet snow had frosted all the windows and turned the streets below into dirty slush. I wondered if I would ever find a cab home that evening. I was about to call when the phone rang and, much to my surprise, it was my sister Helen calling from Auburn, New York. She sounded frantic.

"Hello, hello, Olga," she screamed. I have some terrible news. Ma was killed a few hours ago in a horrible automobile accident. She's dead. Ma's dead. Dead. You've got to come home."

"Ma's dead?" I asked incredulously. "How could this happen? She was so young. Who was driving? Whose fault was it?" I didn't want to believe her.

"Ma was driving," Helen replied, "and she hit a patch of ice on top of the hill on Case Avenue. By accident, she pressed the gas pedal with full force instead of braking and the car went out of control, smashing straight into a huge tree."

There were no seat belts at that time, and her chest impacted the steering wheel with such force, it broke her ribs, causing one to pierce her heart. She died instantly. My father was sitting next to her but was not seriously injured. He was taken to the hospital and stayed there for a few days. He never saw Ma again because she was

1

buried before he was well enough to leave the hospital. All her life Ma wanted to own a car and learn how to drive. When she finally could be independent and go wherever she liked, fate stepped in. She died at the age of fifty-two on November 19, 1955, one week after she received her driver's license.

"Helen, I'll take the first plane I can catch," I said. "Can you have someone meet me in Syracuse to drive me to Auburn?"

That was no problem, so I made reservations for an early morning flight the next day. I was in a state of semi-shock, with memories of my mother collecting in my brain like so many scattered pieces of life. I could think of nothing else. I couldn't even cry.

Arriving home the following morning, I was led into the living room where my mother was laying in an open casket. Many of her friends were there, as well as Catharine Parsell, my English teacher in high school who was also a dear friend. I just stood there looking at my poor, dead mother, unable to fully accept that she was gone. My head was buzzing and I wanted to cry. I kept staring down at my mother's sweet, gentle face, imagining her alive. She was so still, so white. She was always in motion when she was alive. I couldn't bear to think of her closed casket slowly descending into a dark, brown hole, where she would rest forever. There were so many things we had yet to do together. We needed more time. Why? Why? Why did this have to happen?

I must have been standing there for a long time when I felt someone's arm around me. It was Catharine, silently telling me she understood. Tears began to well up and I started to cry. That gentle touch of kindness released all my pent-up feelings and opened me up. My two sisters, Helen and Anne, were there, and we went into the next room to talk. How strange it felt to be in this place, our childhood home, under these conditions.

The funeral was the following day. After the services, we went to the hospital to visit Papa. He was sad, but stoic. He had a way of jutting out his jaw when he was on the verge of crying, and this was one of those moments. He really loved Ma but never knew how to show it. He kept repeating, "Too bad. Too bad." He was unable to communicate his feelings to us. Instead, he hovered over his own private

My grandparents with their 7 children. My mother is third from the right. Photo taken in the Ukraine.

world of fear and loss and sadness, imprisoned in the finality of it. I put my arms around him and thought I saw a tear. "I'm all right. I'm all right," he insisted. I realized he was trying to convince himself, as well as us, that everything was going to be all right. But things weren't all right. They had never been right, because my father was a heavy drinker and we were all affected by his alcoholic personality.

I'd never known my father to break down and cry, and I often wondered if he did so all alone in the privacy of home. After Ma died, he was very lonely but never complained. He returned to the comfortable routine of hard work. I returned to New York and my sister Anne left for Wappingers Falls, where she lived. That left Helen, who lived nearby, to be there for him.

So many old memories came back during the weeks following Ma's death. I kept visualizing her in perpetual-motion mode, digging in her flower beds, weeding the vegetable garden, cooking a big Sunday dinner, washing laundry in the ancient washing machine, cleaning the house, and never sitting down to relax. I invited her once to visit me in New York City, and she stayed for five days. The

My Ukrainian parents, Katarzyna and Wasyl, on their wedding day, October 13, 1923. She was eighteen; he was twenty-six

city frightened her; she would always put her arm through mine, huddling close to me, as we walked the streets. I felt we had reversed roles—I was now the protective mother and she the helpless child. It made me feel very strange. We saw three Broadway shows. She loved them all. This was a whole new world for her, and I was happy she had experienced the thrill of it. Little did I know that within a year she would die. Then the tears would roll down my cheeks, and I would realize she was really gone.

The role my mother played in my life expanded as I grew older. Though she was no longer living, those early childhood years made a silent impact on me. She never demanded I excel; I wanted to. She never insisted I do things her way, because she was always self-conscious about her lack of education and refinement. All she ever asked of us was to do our best. She had no exaggerated expectations, and I never felt pressured by her. I evolved through exposure and experience. We never had mother-daughter talks, no bonding, no affection. But I knew she loved me dearly. I learned at an early age to do everything myself, including finding my own way in life. My mother threw me into focus simply by leaving me alone. I didn't appreciate it at the time, but as I look back I realize the vast ripple-effect one person can cause. Through her simple and genuine respect for my gifts, her intuitive support, and her ability to let go, she helped form me in her own silent way.

Ma was always in charge of our family. She could do everything. She cooked home-made bread from scratch, mixing dough the night before, covering it with a white dish towel to rise, and the following morning forming balls of dough in the bread pans. The smell of Ma's homemade bread baking was like some secret ingredient released by heat to tantalize us. When the bread was ready, we would slice thick pieces and spread butter on the hot, crusty slices.

On holidays she would make special, puffy, cookies cooked in oil and sprinkled with powdered sugar. Sundays it was Ma's boiled chicken, fresh from the clucking chicken coop in back of the house. Ma always amazed us. She knew just how to grab the chicken and with a quick twist of its neck, instantly kill our squawking meal. She would pluck all its feathers, clean out the insides, and bring the ready-to-cook naked chicken into the kitchen, all in a matter of minutes.

Ma also had a green thumb. Our home was surrounded with flower beds until she could find no more room. Roses were her specialty. She knew all about pruning, preparing the soil, and watering. She learned how when she was a young girl on the farm in the Ukraine. Somehow, she also found time to grow a complete vegetable garden. We always had fresh potatoes, tomatoes, green beans, carrots, and cucumbers. She even found time to sew most of our clothes. Disciplining us fell on her as well. Every Saturday she would remind us it was clean-the-house day. The three of us would vacuum, mop, and dust the house. It took all Saturday morning.

Ma was no great beauty. She was short and stocky and weighed one hundred sixty pounds most of her life. She often tried to lose weight, but couldn't. She had no waistline and was quite bosomy. Her face was kind and gentle, and whenever she laughed, her deep hazel eyes would light up and twinkle. Her hair was dark brown. She would twirl strands into little pin curls that became soft waves when she removed the bobby pins. Sometimes she would pull all her hair back and form a bun at the back of her neck. Ma's and Pa's wedding portrait hangs in my home today with the two of them standing, staring at the camera with very serious expressions. He is quite handsome, lean, and a little taller than Ma. It's one of the few times in his life he wore a suit. Ma wore a long white dress with a floor length veil bordered with beautiful white flowers that also circled her face. She carried a simple bridal bouquet of assorted white flowers with satin ribbons floating down over her gown.

In 1938, Ma decided to follow Pa's lead and become an American citizen. She enrolled in night school citizenship classes and attended for several months. Many an evening I sat with her, going over English lessons and she, in turn, taught me Ukrainian. She received her citizenship papers later that year, fulfilling a lifelong dream. How proudly she stood with the other applicants and recited the Pledge of Allegiance!

Even with all the problems of living with Pa, Ma still managed to keep the family together. Every Saturday morning she demanded his pay, which in those days was paid in cash. He would obediently give it to her after taking out enough for his weekend binging. Ma paid all the bills and took care of the other finances. While Pa was drinking a good portion of his paycheck, Ma, who also worked, was saving as much of hers as she could. Miraculously, she was able to put a three-thousand-dollar down-payment to buy our home and paid the mortgage throughout my growing years. There was a little mortgage payment book she would pull out of the drawer when the mortgage man came around regularly to collect payments. Ma paid cash and would carefully count out the dollars, nickels, and dimes so the amount was absolutely correct.

When the three of us grew older, it was time to add another story to our home. It was decided that since the mortgage was growing smaller, we could finally have our own rooms. What excitement when the building began! The stairs that used to lead to the attic would now open up to three bedrooms and a family room. I chose the room with a window overlooking the Kowal's backyard and, in the distance, the fields and countryside where I used to walk alone. What joy to have a room all to myself!

Ma was still working full time at the rope company when she died. She liked earning her own money; it gave her a sense of independence. I always remember her taking the bus to work or walking quite a long distance. She never complained. She always remembered how hard life was in the Old Country.

Katarzyna Yarko, my mother, came to the United States when she was sixteen, speaking very little English. She came from a small farm community near Kiev in the Ukraine. Her family was poor, and everyone worked long hours on the farm. She was the second of seven children. Ma always talked about saving enough money to help bring her sisters and brothers to America. Though it took many years, she managed to do that with three siblings, which was quite an accomplishment with all her other responsibilities.

My father came to America when he was sixteen years old, ten years ahead of my mother. His passport identified him, "Wasyl Mysliwczuk, born February 2, 1896, arrived in New York aboard the ship Victoria May 25, 1912." He came alone. He spoke no English, and he had no friends. He left Russia-dominated Ukraine at a time of social and political turmoil that eventually led to revolution and the tsar's overthrow during World War I. His journey ended life as he had known it. Everything that was familiar disappeared, as his ship to America left behind forever all that was familiar—home, family, and friends. It must have been painful and frightening. He was left with only his boyhood memories. At sixteen he was almost a man ready to join the army. Could that have been the reason his parents sent him to America? We never knew, because my father refused to talk about it. The only link to his past I now have is his passport, ninety-one years old, battered and yellowed with age.

It didn't take long for my father to meet many of the other Ukrainians on board the ship. He was friendly, shaking hands, smiling,

and starting conversations. They
liked him and suggested he go
to Massachusetts with them so
he wouldn't be alone. By the
time he saw the Statue of Lib-
erty and landed on Ellis Island,
my father was ready to start his
new life in America. He decided
to go to Massachusetts and soon
became part of the Ukrainian
community. His new friends
helped him find a place to live
and brought him to the woolen
mills to find a job. He was soon
working long hours as a weaver
of carpets. Life must have been

Anna, Helen, and Olga in 1935

bearable enough. He was young and handsome and was quickly
learning the English language. When he was twenty-four he decided
to move to Auburn, New York.

Ma met Pa about a year after she arrived in this country. It must
have been love at first sight, because they were married soon afterwards, on October 13, 1923, when she was only eighteen. He was
twenty-six. Within a year their first child, Anna, was born, followed
by Helen two years later, and finally by me, Olga the baby, two years
after her. That was our family.

I always wondered about my grandparents, whom I never knew.
Their names appeared on my parent's marriage certificate. Harry
Mysliwczuk and Palagia Wityk were my father's parents, and Michael
Yarko and Anna Dolishna were my mother's. When my father left
for America, his parents stayed in the Ukraine. Unknown to them
at the time, they would never see their son again. This parting lasted
a lifetime. Over the years they never communicated, and my father
never spoke about them. It was as though his life didn't exist before,
and it all began on American soil.

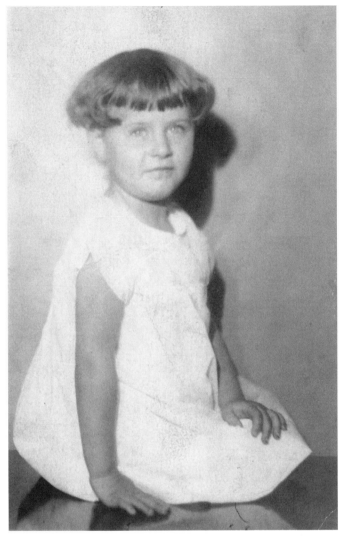

5 year old, Olga. This is my favorite "little girl" picture. My mother would cut my "stylish" hair with two different bowls on my head. This is the story of my life.

As a little girl, I used to be my father's favorite. Whenever he had a little too much to drink and tried to hug or kiss me, I would run away as fast as I could. We were quite poor. These were the thirties, the depression years. My father was laid off and then worked for the W.P.A. Prohibition was in full swing, but Pa made moonshine in the basement. My sister got the measles at this time and we were quarantined. My father had to live outside the home in order to go to work, but he would often sneak back to see us. "Olha, Anna, Helen, come here. I have some treats for you." We would run to the window, and he would hand each of us a brown paper bag with candies, cookies, and fruit. He was very thoughtful to us during that time. We thanked him and waved goodbye.

Eventually, things got better and both my parents found jobs. Ma worked at the Columbian Rope Company making twine. She constantly smelled like nice new rope. Pa worked in the foundry at the International Harvester Company. He was very strong and never missed a day of work, even with burns on both arms. Ma worked days and Pa worked nights, which left only the weekends for us to be together. However, we were never together. Pa lived two lives: his work life and his drinking life. He would get his pay on Friday night and go to the bar. On Saturday and Sunday he would be there when the bar opened. Even when I was a little five year old, Ma used to send me there to urge him out and guide him home. He always staggered but flailed his arms for me to let go, because he insisted he could walk by himself. I remember being quite young; how embarrassing it was for me to walk into that smelly, dank, bar, tug at his shirt tail, and plead with him to come home.

"Go away," he would say, "I go nowhere. I stay here!"

"But Papa, Mama wants you home," I insisted.

I always stood by his bar stool until he was ready to leave. All the men laughed loudly at me and at him. I was so ashamed. (It seemed that all the Ukrainian men on Case Avenue drank too much.) When we reached home, Pa always asked me to remove his shoes and socks. Oh! How I hated the damp smell of his dirty socks. I would warm up some food for him and sit with him while he ate, slurped, and burped.

Over the years Pa never changed; he continued his weekend drinking and weekday working. Whenever any of his friends came over, the first thing he would do was bring out the bottle of whiskey and the shot glasses and insist, "Drink! Drink! Good whiskey." Ma would always be embarrassed because Pa didn't single out his friends. He had whiskey for everyone, even my mother's friends when they dropped in.

Namisniak's bar was still his favorite weekend activity, and weekend after weekend, month after month, year after year, he followed the same routine. Even as a child, I couldn't understand what he liked about that dark, dreary bar that always smelled of old beer and stale pretzels. I can still remember that long, mahogany bar with all the men standing and leaning against it because there were no bar stools. "Another whiskey, Joe," my father would order as I tugged harder on his coat tails. "Okay, okay," he said slurring his words. "This will be my last drink." When he finished, he staggered home with me running behind him, my short, little legs barely able to keep up.

The next day, sitting on the porch steps talking to Pa, I would ask, "Why do you drink so much, Papa? It's bad for you and you act different and you talk different."

"You don't understand, Olha. You don't understand," he would always say.

I didn't ever tell him how ashamed I was by his behavior or how nice it would be if we could do things together as a family. I couldn't reach him. I do know, today, how much I missed sober hugs and kisses, a father I could talk to about my needs, a parent who was supportive, understanding, and kind. How many times did I hold back my tears as I watched him stagger down the street in a drunken stupor?

Neighbors would slyly call from their porches, "Hey, Cowboy, how ya doin'?"

He would laugh and answer, "Aw right, aw right." It was humiliating to see him that way, and from those early memories I can still feel the shame.

Ma must have been very sad and lonely deep inside. She and Pa had no loving relationship, and we never saw them hugging, kissing, or holding hands. They were like two people who simply lived in the same house, going through the same daily routine. I do remember, however, she had a friend, Mike Bazar, who used to take us on Sunday drives while my father drank in the bar. He was kind and gentle towards Ma and we all knew he secretly loved her. I used to ask Ma why she didn't divorce Pa and marry Mike. She would blush and say it wasn't possible. I can still recall, as a small child, going on those long Sunday drives. I would fall asleep on my mother's soft bosom to the steady hum of the car engine and not awaken until we reached home. Mike even took us to Syracuse to the State Fair one year.

Those were the kind of togetherness memories I never had with my father. We didn't even go to the movies together, share a picnic, take a walk, or play horseshoes. The only event he ever attended with us was a Ukrainian wedding at the Ukrainian Hall. How he drank! And how he danced! But he didn't dance with Ma.

TWO

My Auburn Childhood

Life during the Depression

Growing up in Auburn, New York had its advantages. It was a small city, population 36,000, located in the middle of the state in an area called the Finger Lakes Region. Miraculously, nature had formed five finger-shaped lakes that look like an outspread hand. Owasco Lake was the finger lake that Auburn touched. Going to the lake in the summer with Ma was a special treat, because bordering it was a big amusement park. When my sisters and I weren't swimming, we'd dress and go for a ride on the merry-go-round. I always ran to make sure I sat on the "horse that moved up and down" as it went around. Or we would jump on the Bumper Cars and pretend we were grown-ups crashing. The Ferris Wheel scared me because the chairs swayed, and when you reached the top and started to descend you felt as though you were floating in mid-air. Sometimes we would have our pictures taken in a booth behind a heavy curtain. When we were hungry, there were plenty of snack bars that sold puffs of cotton candy, creamy ice cream cones, popcorn, hot dogs, and soda pop. On Saturday night there was a dance at the Lake Pavilion with live music. Sometimes we would stay a little later than usual and watch the dancers slow dance and jitterbug. Years later I joined in.

When I was a child, Auburn seemed very big to me. Our business district had a mix of retail stores like Woolworth's, Kresge's and Hislop's. There were assorted office buildings, a drugstore with a soda fountain (a teenage hangout), and three movie theaters. I remember selling popcorn at the Capitol Theatre the day Pearl Harbor was bombed. Suddenly, out of nowhere, two new customers ran up the stairs screaming, "The Japanese have bombed Pearl Harbor. The Japanese have bombed Pearl Harbor." They ran up the stairs and into the dark theatre. Within minutes customers came running out of the movie in a state of shock. "Did the Japs really bomb Pearl Harbor?" they asked in disbelief. The manager came down and announced to all of us that it was true. He had just heard the news on the radio. I don't remember what movie was playing that day, but it was probably a good Western, the Three Stooges, or a double feature. The fancy Palace Theater carried the best, the latest, Hollywood had to offer. That's where I fell in love with Tyrone Power and Cary Grant. And that's where I saw every Shirley Temple movie made. Although we were poor, each Sunday we were given a dime for the movie and a nickel for a double dip ice cream cone. I was ecstatic when my mother bought me a pink ruffled Shirley Temple dress. I still remember the childhood joy of anything-Shirley Temple!

My birth name was Olga Mysliwczuk. We spoke Ukrainian at home, so I knew very little English when I entered first grade. Away from home, alone for the first time, a whole new world opened up for me. I was on my own. That first day our teacher asked each one in our class to stand as our name was called. When it was my turn she could not pronounce my last name. I stood up slowly, eyes downcast, as she struggled with it, "Olga Mysli, Mysloo, Mysliz, Myslizook." My face turned bright red, and the whole class laughed. This provoked a strong, new feeling of shame in me. As I sat down, I vowed they would never laugh at me again! Unfortunately, the same experience repeated itself each school year. Every teacher struggled with my last name. Even at college, years later, I flushed with embarrassment as my name was called. Everyone in the class turned around to see who owned "that" name. Finally, when I graduated from college and was living in New York I changed my name legally to Ollie Myles. I now felt anglicized; I belonged.

While I was growing up, we lived at 23 Case Avenue. We only had one floor, with a kitchen, dining room, living room, and one bedroom. We had a big yard and a cellar. We had a coal bin in the cellar where coal would be delivered down the chute. The furnace was also down there. It warmed the entire house. We spent many hours playing in the basement because it was cozy and warm. However, in the winter it would burn out in the early morning and the house would be freezing cold. Every morning Ma would burn some logs in the kitchen stove to warm up the room. Our kitchen was small. In it was a white metal table and chairs, a stove that was black with an oven that cooked home made bread, an ice box that received a block of ice regularly, and a washing machine. Years and years of washing was done in that machine. We would help by ringing out the clothes with a manual ringer right in the middle of the kitchen. The dining room was only used for holidays and those rare occasions when we would have a guest or relative for a meal. The living room was used when we had guests, which was not very often. It had a plush couch with two matching chairs, a velvet painting, and some of Ma's plants. We all shared the same bedroom, one bed at each end of the room. My parents slept in one bed, and the three of us in the other. Occasionally I would sleep between Ma and Pa. In the middle of the night I could hear Pa pleading with Ma for something. He would then lay on top of her and grunt and groan. How the bed squeaked as it went up and down. I was terrified he was hurting Ma.

"Stop pounding on Ma." I screamed, "Get off her! Get off her!"

I was only three years old and knew nothing about sex, but it was the last time I was allowed to sleep in their bed.

Pa always used to say to us, "An honest day's work for an honest day's pay." I never saw my parents idle, a trait I inherited. He was handy and could repair or build simple things. He planted and took care of eight fruit trees around the front yard. We had peaches, apples, plums, and cherries all season long. He also built a large grape arbor with blue grapes at one end and white grapes at the

Our home in Auburn where I lived the first 18 years of my life

other. There was a glider to sit on in the shade of the grape leaves and eat grapes throughout the summer.

We never had a car or a telephone. We walked, rode our bicycles, or took the bus everywhere. Pa's only transportation was his bicycle, which he rode back and forth to work. He used to put on a trouser clamp to prevent his pants from getting stuck in the bicycle sprocket, and he always wore his cap. How I used to envy the kids at school whose parents would pick them up in expensive cars! They all spoke perfect English and dressed in beautiful clothes. I couldn't help comparing them to my immigrant parents, who worked in factories and spoke broken English. I wasn't angry about this, just ashamed. I was even ashamed of myself for feeling like this. I loved my mother very much. She was a good woman, kind, loving, (though not demonstrative), and hard-working. Her three children were her whole life. My father used to drive her crazy because of his drinking. He used to yell at her and hit her and my sisters, and I would try to physically pull him away from her. I remember one Saturday night Pa came home, smelly and drunk, after drinking at the bar all day. Within five minutes Ma was screaming at him in Ukrainian about his drinking and what a bad husband he was. This time Pa screamed back at her raising his arm to strike. Ma grabbed the closest thing to her, a kitchen chair, and threw it straight at him. Luckily he dodged it, so she picked up a rolling pin and threw that still screaming loudly. My sisters and I were huddled in a corner, terrified someone would get hurt, and were glad the rolling pin missed him too. Finally, my father ran out of the kitchen door and down the driveway with my mother close behind waving the kitchen broom like a witch with her favorite tool. She finally came back in the house, and an hour or so later Pa sulked back and quietly went to bed. They didn't speak to each other for a week.

Growing up in a Ukrainian neighborhood meant everyone attended the Greek Catholic church. Everyone but us. My parents withdrew from the church when I was little. We were told Pa was an usher and a pillar of Saint Peter and Paul church. He was accused by one of the priests of stealing money from the basket. He was so humiliated, he left the church forever. It was later discovered that the accusing priest himself had taken the money. Because of this incident, I never had any "church experience." I always felt like a sinner doomed. I'll never forget the description of Hell that Helen Kowal, our next door neighbor, described to me. She showed me a picture in one of her holy books that depicted snakes and demons devouring people in a raging fire. God, that was a nightmare for me for years! I was about eight years old at the time. "But I don't want to go to Hell!" I screamed and ran home sobbing. There was no one home to console me.

I did a lot of daydreaming when I was young. I was pretty much a loner then. I used to take long walks by myself, often arriving at my own private meadow. I would lie in the grass and sing to myself. I'd go down by the river and watch it flow and listen to it gurgle. I would dream about the future. I would marry a nice man who would sweep me off my feet. He would open up all the pent-up love I could never share with my family. I vowed never to marry a man who drank because of all those years with Pa. He disgusted me. Love was not a word we used. Sharing, praise, reassurances, consoling, understanding, supporting, all forms of nurture that we never experienced. I can't blame Ma or Pa. They were always working to keep the bare essentials of life coming to us, food on the table, a roof over our heads, and clothes on our backs. That's how they showed they loved us. Our physical needs were taken care of, but we were emotionally empty. I grew up very needy requiring constant reassurances, a compliment, or a hug to validate me. I still do after all these years.

Winters were cold in upstate New York. The snow was often so deep we needed to shovel it out of the driveway in order to get to school. I remember the icicles that formed on the outside of our roof edges like so many stalactites. We used to break one off and lick it like a long, thin lollipop. The milkman used to deliver milk in the winter and put it on the stoop outside our kitchen. The below-freezing weather popped the cap of the glass milk bottle and left about an inch of ice milk above it. How we loved that! When Spring finally arrived we were ready to see the snow disappear. It melted, layer after layer, until patches of bare ground became visible.

Soon Spring would be here and Ma's gardens would begin to bloom again. That she could do everything and still work full time at the rope factory was taken for granted. Only years later, as an adult, did I appreciate her tireless energy for work. She maintained a sense of order and security within the family, so we were not afraid, even on screaming weekends with Pa. Sometimes, however, we were frightened because Ma couldn't control her agony and frustration and would wind herself out of control.

We were expected to be clean and tidy, do the dishes after meals, and complete our chores every day. When she went to night school to study for her citizenship papers, Pa did the babysitting. It was the only time we had his complete, sober attention. He taught us some songs we had never heard before, and he sang them with great gusto. When Ma learned about this, she was furious calling them "Bar Room" songs. They seemed innocent enough to us, but I've forgotten all the naughty ones. This simple little tune, however, has stayed with me all my life:

Na walitzka scriptka hraya; moya mater na puskaya;
Pusti, pusti, moia mater; troshka saubi pu hilati.

Translation:

In the distance violins are playing; mother will not let us go;
She will let us go! She will let us go! She wants to dance herself.

I always felt Ma saw me as an extension of herself. I was the brightest of her three children, and she used to praise me when I showed her my report cards. "Olha, that is very good. You must always work hard, so you go to college someday." School was very easy for me, and I soon learned how rewarding it was to excel. My teachers didn't openly favor me, but they let me know when we were alone how proud they were of me. "I love school," I would always say. "It's easy for me." I never wanted to miss a day, and even if I was sick, I would try to hide it so I wouldn't be kept home. One time I went to school with a bad cough, and when I was at the blackboard I sneezed so hard it wet the entire board. I couldn't stop coughing. The teacher took me out in the hallway, helped me with my coat and hat, and sent me home. Ma had to call the doctor, and after examining me he announced, "Young lady. You have whooping cough. You will remain in bed for at least two weeks." My heart was broken because I would miss so much school. I had a fever and the cough persisted, but in two weeks I was back at school.

My two sisters, Anna and Helen, used to ask me to help them with their homework if there was something they couldn't do. It made me feel important, because I was so much younger and their schoolwork was easy for me. We played together until Anna was about sixteen and boys entered the picture. She decided to go to secretarial school, and when she graduated from high school, a job was easy to find. She started dating Paul Panson, a nice Ukrainian man, which eventually led to their marriage and four children. My sister Helen and I were left together, and we formed a bond that has lasted all these years. She studied to be a nurse and practised nursing all her life. She dated and eventually married John Pasternak, another good Ukrainian man. They also have four children.

That scenario was not for me. I wanted to be independent, and at eleven earned money picking fruits and vegetables for the local farmers on weekends and summer vacations. At fourteen, I

Family portrait, 1944. Anna is now married to Paul Panson

sorted fishhooks in a fishhook factory. It was the most tedious task
I had ever done. Fortunately, the office manager decided I would
be more useful in her office and after two weeks transferred me.
I was thrilled! At sixteen, I was a playground counselor, and at
seventeen, I was a stock girl at Gertrude Herron, the best retail
store in town. I used to love opening boxes of merchandise and
hanging up the clothes. It was like Christmas every day. Mrs.
Herron gave me fashion information on each piece, and I soon

learned to recognize designers' looks. By the end of summer I purchased a new red coat to bring to college with me. Little did I know at the time that my entire future career in fashion had started right there.

I was always eager to be the best, and during my four years of high school every minute was filled with schoolwork or a frenzy of extra-curricular activities. I was a class officer. I loved sports and played soccer, softball, and basketball. I was a cheerleader for several years and for two years won the foul shooting championship of Auburn, consistently shooting twenty-four or twenty-five out of twenty-five balls. My father cherished my trophies and newspaper articles and used to bring them to the bar. "That's my Olga," he would proudly announce and pass the articles up and down the bar. I also played the violin in the school orchestra, squeaking my way through six years of study. I was a mediocre violinist, but my father loved the violin and patiently sat nearby listening to me practice. How he could stand those early do-re-mi notes, hour after hour, amazed me.

I was the female lead in our senior class play, "The Ghost Train."

In addition to music, I was interested in the Drama Club. I desperately wanted the lead in our senior play, "The Ghost Train." I memorized the role and practised for hours and hours. Competing for the part were several girls from the east side of town. When it was my turn to audition, I wasn't nervous, but I may have "overacted." We weren't told who would have the lead until a few days later. I was thrilled to be selected but even more excited when the play was over and I hadn't forgotten my lines. At about the same time, the school staff appointed me editor-in-chief of our yearbook, a position I eagerly wanted. The staff and I worked all year pulling together the photographs, activities, clubs, sports, teachers, and endless details until we were finally finished. I proudly wrote the editorial, one page long, full of the promise of tomorrow. It concludes with these words:

We cannot teach the world how to live, or how to live in peace, until as individuals in a nation we have demonstrated that we have learned ourselves how to pursue and how to preserve the happiness which has been our constitutional privilege for so many generations.

I was editor-in-chief of our Class of '46 year book

I occasionally take the book down from my bookshelf to once again remind myself of the little Ukrainian girl determined to do her best even at an early age.

My English teacher, Catharine Parsell, became my mentor. She recognized something in me that led to a friendship lasting a lifetime. But for her, I might have landed in Cortland State Teacher's College and become a gym teacher. I shudder. I was so naïve. She was determined I go to Cornell University, and from freshman year through graduation she encouraged me to excel in all my subjects. I wrote additional essays and read a number of books she recommended. We would discuss everything. My French teacher, Charlotte Katzmar, was her best friend, and by the time I graduated, I spoke fluent French and read novels in French. Miss Parsell

Catharine Parsell, my English teacher, was my mentor during high school. Without her help. I may never have achieved my future success.

used to invite me to her home to teach me manners, table manners in particular. "Olga," she would say, "this is how you properly set the table. Forks go on the left, spoons and knives on the right". We would have tea, and she would teach me what to do with the spoon after stirring the tea. She taught me how to break my roll one piece at a time and how to cut my meat and place the knife and fork properly on the plate. "No elbows on the table," she would instruct. "Keep your hands in your lap." After a few lessons, I set the table and we practiced our meal-manners.

Miss Parsell helped throughout my four years of high school, encouraging, praising, and guiding me. She even saw me through my first big love, during the giddiness of first bloom when she shared my joy and later when he found someone else and she comforted me. His name was Al Johnson, and we dated for almost a year, holding

My high school senior yearbook graduation picture. I was an honor student and was accepted by Cornell for Fall of 1946.

hands from class to class, lingering by our lockers together, going to the football and basketball games, watching movies, and sitting on the glider on our front porch necking. The farthest we ever dared was long kisses. I was stricken when, out of nowhere, he "dropped" me. He never explained why, but my heart was broken. I found out, subsequently, that he was dating one of the "fast" girls in class and obviously had discovered sex. It hurt so much to see them together. A few years after graduation, I heard Al had died of cancer.

THREE

Far above Cayuga's Waters

Four Years at Cornell

By the time senior year began, I was immersed in thoughts of Cornell. Miss Parsell helped me fill out my application for admittance, and since that was the only university I wanted to attend, all my hopes were focused there. One hundred fifty of us would be accepted out of two thousand or more applicants for the College of Human Ecology. It was a state-endowed college, and my mother was able to afford it since the tuition was paid. My father always thought I should get married and have children, but it was my mother who was thrilled that one of her daughters might be college-educated.

"Why waste all that money for nothing?" he would ask.

My mother would always reply, "I will pay every penny I earn by myself to send Olha to college. You can drink up your money. I don't need it!"

As Spring approached, I finally heard from Cornell. They would be interviewing prospective students early in March, and I was among the group selected. I quickly called Miss Parsell, "I'm going for an interview; I'm going for an interview," I screamed with joy. By now I was jumping up and down and could hardly contain myself.

"I'm so proud of you, Olga; you've worked very hard for this," she said happily.

We both felt how special that moment was, but it was just the beginning. All I did for the next few weeks was plan what I would wear and what I would say. We practiced mock interviews, and I felt fully prepared by the time "the day" arrived. The interview took place in Syracuse, about twenty-five miles east of Auburn. I wore a cream twin sweater set with a navy pleated skirt and a strand of pearls. My hair was dark brown, newly shampooed, and fell to my shoulders. I wore no makeup, only light lipstick. The interview took over an hour, and I felt good about it when we finished.

"You will hear from us sometime late April or May," the woman interviewer advised me, shaking my hand vigorously.

I reviewed the interview in my head as we drove back home. I'm glad I had all those extracurricular activities. She spent some time on that. Straight A's scholastically; they expected that. All the required courses. On and on I went. From that day on I prayed.

By early May I was beginning to think they had rejected me and I would soon be notified. Then "the letter" arrived. I was so afraid I wouldn't be accepted, I didn't tell anyone I had received it. I sat in my room for several hours, imagining projected one-act dramas of "Life without Cornell." "Enough of this," I finally told myself and slowly opened the envelope. As I unfolded the letter I could see, "We are happy to inform you that you have been accepted in the College of Human Ecology at Cornell University for the Fall Semester, September 8, 1946" — thump! THUMP! thump! THUMP! My heart was beating so fast I could hardly breathe. I have to share this right away! I called Miss Parsell and excitedly told her the good news:

"We did it! We did it! I've just been accepted at Cornell!"

She was almost as happy as I was. "Hooray for you! I knew you could do it! I knew it!"

When my mother came home from work I told her the good news. She hugged me and with tears in her eyes whispered, "Olha, my little Olha, how happy I am for you! Your life will be so much better because you will be educated and have a college degree. How I wish I had been born in this country, to go to school and learn like you."

I always remembered her joy at that moment, and knew I had to succeed, not for one, but for two of us. That memory stayed with me all my life, nudging my drive and determination. How I wish she could have lived longer to see the results.

During this same time I began to feel lost inside me, empty and incomplete. There was something missing in my life. I knew it had to do with God, and spirituality, and church. For months I tried not to think of it, but I soon learned I couldn't control those feelings. All I could do was feel them. It was a slow awakening, very private and not shared with anyone. I was too busy with all my schoolwork and activities. Then one day, returning home from school on the bus, I decided to get off downtown. It was as though I was beckoned, God speaking to my heart and not my head. I walked a few blocks to St. Mary's church, rang the doorbell, and was led into the rectory.

A few minutes later a priest came in and introduced himself, "I'm Father Dennis Hickey, and who might you be, and what can I do for you?"

For a moment I wanted to run out the door. What was I doing there anyway? My feet were holy-glued to the floor.

"Father, my name is Olga Myslichuk (we "anglicized" it a bit in high school), and if you can convince me the Catholic Church is the one true religion I will convert to Catholicism!"

He chuckled. "I'll take you on," he said, "but you will have to come here weekly and study your catechism just as the children do."

So for almost a year we worked together one-on-one. At the end, I found myself not only intellectually converted but also zealous. I attended mass and received communion daily. I read spiritual books, attended weekend retreats, and when my sister, Helen, asked me about becoming a Catholic, I encouraged her. My religious beliefs were very important to me from the beginning. When I attended Cornell, Father Cleary was the Catholic priest who encouraged me to join the Newman Club and become involved in the Campus church. It was through Father Cleary that I met Monsignor Fulton J. Sheen and one of his converts, Claire Booth Luce. This was years later when I lived in New York City. We were both invited to the Luce's magnificent home for dinner. Henry and Clare Booth Luce were the Power Couple of the era. Famous internationally, he was the founder and president of Time, Inc., which published *Time* and *Life* magazines. They were among the most influential magazines in the country. Claire Booth Luce was an author and playwright. Her most famous book, *The Women*, was made into a Broadway play starring Katherine Hepburn. It was later produced as a movie. She was also the United States envoy to the Vatican and American

Father Cleary was our Cornell chaplain

ambassador to Italy. I was impressed, and that queasy-little-Ukrainian-girl feeling momentarily touched me. At the dinner table I was no longer intimidated, because I knew I could hold my own in any conversation. Henry Luce sat at the head of the table and Claire at the other end. Floating on the other two sides were Father Cleary and me. Mrs. Luce talked and talked and talked, totally dominating the conversation. She was fascinating, and knew so much about so many different subjects like politics, travel, problems in Europe, world leaders. We heard very little from Mr. Luce, Father Cleary, or me. It was my first experience with a powerful woman insensitive to those around her.

When I was in high school I never dreamed that in the future I would meet such prominent people. I just kept studying and participating, and before I knew it high school graduation day arrived. We all assembled in our black caps and gowns, ready to march down the aisle in the auditorium to our seats. Several of us had seats on stage because we were part of the program.

As I sat there, I looked at Deane Turner, our valedictorian, and thought to myself, "He's one of the smartest students in our class. He'll probably become a nuclear scientist."

Bob Melone, our class president and salutatorian, had an outgoing personality and everyone liked him. "He might go into politics."

I was third highest, scholastically, and was getting very excited about entering Cornell in the Fall. We all delivered commencement speeches or "readings" during the program My mother, my sister Helen, and Catharine Parsell came to see me graduate. My father did not. He missed out on so much in our lives over the years because of his weekend binges. At the time I didn't realize it, but as I grew older I believed part of his drinking was to drown out the memories of his family in the Old Country. It was too painful not knowing. There were moments I would catch him staring out in space, and I would wonder, "Is he thinking of his mother? His father? Any sisters or brothers?" The fact that he never had contact with them must have left an emptiness in his heart, and whatever innermost thoughts lay dormant in his memory died with him, never having had a life of their own.

The day for leaving home at eighteen to begin college finally arrived. It started with Freshman Camp, an orientation for newcomers to Cornell. We were bussed out in the woods a few miles away and assigned cabins and roommates. It was get-acquainted time for two days. The counselors gave us information about the university, but it was mostly togetherness with walks, and talks, and friendliness. At night a fire was built, and we all sat around it roasting marshmallows and singing songs. It was a happy way to begin our new journey.

Then school began. I was unprepared for the initial college experience, because I was not accustomed to lectures and taking notes. Public school never taught us that. We learned how to take notes on our own, but I still felt totally unprepared that first day walking into a huge lecture hall filled with hundreds of students. This was quite a change from little East High School in Auburn, New York. When the professor began his lecture promptly on the hour, we all opened our notebooks and started writing. I didn't lift my head once because I was afraid I would miss something important, that one sentence that might be the answer to getting an A in the course instead of a B. One hour and pages of notes later, the lecture was over.

By contrast, the next day my classes were all in the College of Human Ecology, where I began my journey into the world of textiles and clothing. After a few semesters of basic classes like "The History of Fashion," "Identifying Fibers in Materials," and "The Proper Fit of Garments," we started construction of a dress for our own bodies. This taught us how to drape fabric on a form and end up with a pattern of different pieces. We also learned how to make patterns from sketches, how to grade patterns into sizes 6 through 16, and how to fit and alter garments. When we were taught the art of tailoring, our instructor emphasized the importance of pressing, and under-pressing, the collars and lapels of jackets. This knowledge helped tremendously when, many years later as a buyer for Saks Fifth Avenue and eventually in my own store, I could see a garment on a client and know why it fit incorrectly. I could even pin up a hem in an emergency. My "eye" was constantly being trained.

During those early days at Cornell, I felt a little overwhelmed at first. The students came from around the world, and they impressed me with their knowledge and backgrounds. The girls in the dormitories all seemed so much more sophisticated. Several from New York City had the most beautiful clothes; I couldn't help comparing them to my home-made ones. I became acutely aware of how "small town" I really was, but it didn't take long for me to realize that, in the future, I too would see the world.

It also didn't take long for me to fit into the campus scene once the initial shock subsided. It was 1946 and World War II was over, making our classes full of returning veterans. The men outnumbered the women four to one, because so many veterans made use of the GI Bill of Rights that gave them a free college education. The government passed this piece of legislation to encourage returning veterans to continue their educations, and millions took advantage of the opportunity. They were serious students.

Early in the fall of freshman year, sorority rushing began. The excitement and anticipation among the girls in the dormitory was contagious. "How many invitations did you receive?" "Did you get one from Tri Delt, or Kappa Kappa Gamma, or Theta?" I didn't know one from the other, but I did receive plenty of invitations. We were invited to tea to get acquainted, and if we were asked back for "second viewing," our chances of receiving a bid to join the sorority were good. How I longed to be in a sorority! It was like a stamp of superior approval. As I received a variety of bids to join, I realized in my heart I couldn't accept any of them. My poor mother was struggling to eke out the money for my room and board, and I needed to wait tables and tend desk in the dorm for a little extra income just to stay in college. Sorority life was an extravagance for the "rich girls," and I knew I couldn't afford it. I gulped down that experience only to discover later that my choice to remain "independent" was right. The dormitories, in general, had more privacy and better accommodations.

My dorm room was part of a suite, two rooms connected with a shared bathroom. It was in the front, overlooking a spectacular view of the campus and consisting of four Halls, like a large rectangle with a courtyard in the center. It was reminiscent of buildings in old English movies, constructed in the Georgian style. There was a large, homey living room for entertaining guests and for our dates to wait for us. It was like living with a family. We ate at a specified time for dinner each evening, we shared the communal showers, and we were required to obey evening hours for returning to the dormitory. Each Hall had an adult den mother who saw that rules were obeyed. I lived in Balch Halls for three years and loved every minute.

I kept a diary of my four years at Cornell, and when I read it over again I can't believe that me was ME. During the week, mornings, noons, and nights were filled with classes, activities, and homework. Weekends were for dating. The popular girls (I guess I was one) would have as many as three dates in one evening. Saturday night there were always fraternity parties. I would usually wear a simple slim black dress with high heels and a strand of pearls and start after dorm dinner about 7:00 with one date. Next date would be at 9:00. The last date at about 11:00 was usually a change-into-casual sweater and slacks. It took some maneuvering, but there were times when I would bump right into my next date arriving as I was returning.

"Oops. Hi, Ken. Are you a little early? I need to go to my room for a minute. I'll be right back. Wait for me inside, in the living room." I was a little embarrassed.

Bill, my nine o'clock date, wisecracked, "How do you keep track of us?" And turning to Ken, he remarked, "I guess we go for the same type of girl." Then he looked at me and I could see he was upset. "Good night, Ollie. See you around."

Not too nice, but we girls would laugh hysterically later in the evening in the dorm as we compared our experiences. One Saturday night when I was dating someone regularly, I spent the entire evening with him. "Ollie," he whispered in my ear, "let's go steady." I was really surprised. "I think I'm falling in love with you," he continued, "and I can't stand the thought of anyone else touching you or being with you." This was Saturday night and the entryways were filled with couples kissing good night, gazing into each others' eyes, not able to bear leaving each other. I didn't know what to say, because that was the last thing I wanted as a freshman in college. "I don't think that's a good idea, Bob. You and I should feel free to date other people." He was shocked and hurt. We said good night and he was off. The following weekend I spotted him in the entryway passionately embracing one of my girlfriends. He worked fast.

Willard Straight was the student activity building. I spent many hours there meeting friends and enjoying a cup of coffee or a hot chocolate. It was always full of students and a good place to relax between classes. Barton Hall was used for our periodic Balls, featuring such big bands as Jimmy Dorsey and Tex Beneke with the Meadow Larks. There were football and basketball games, and ice hockey on Lake Beebe. The little town of Ithaca, where Cornell was located, also had plenty of places to occupy us. Bars, restaurants, and movie theaters were supported by the students. I used to love when friends from Auburn visited because it was another world. One of my best friends in high school, Totsie Fernandes, came down to see me because I was anxious to convince her to attend Cornell. She was so bright, so popular, so sweet, and she was voted the most beautiful girl in our senior class. I'm sure she would have been accepted because she had all the scholastic, extra curricular, and leadership qualifications. She never tried, and I've always wondered if she ever regretted her decision. I lost track of her soon after my freshman year, but I did hear she married quite young, had several children, and stayed in Auburn.

I learned from those four years at Cornell how important it was for me to be exposed to a higher education, not only for the schooling, but also to experience the transition from immature high school girl to confident college graduate. All I knew when I entered Cornell was what I had learned in Auburn, New York living with my Ukrainian parents. I was ready for growth. The calibre of people I met and new friendships enriched my life. The discipline of getting A's in my classes fed my pride. The mix of college activities proved my leadership abilities. All this prepared me for a future successful career in fashion and eventually for opening my own business. Without my English teacher's recognition of my potential in high school, none of this would have happened. I would have remained cooped up inside my dreams, wondering all my life why I was so restless deep within, never having blossomed, never having reached for the stars. I believe you should make full use of the gifts God gives you. If not, perpetual frustration will follow. I can't imagine where I would be today if it weren't for my Cornell education, experiences, exposure, and introductions to the interesting people I met.

In addition to the good stuff I also learned some facts of life, particularly at House Party weekends at the fraternities. I was really shocked at the quantity of drinking that went on and the loose morals. Since I never drank anything stronger than a Coke and limited myself to hugs and kisses, I wasn't your typical life-of-the-party. It didn't seem to matter as much during those years because jumping into bed with your date wasn't really expected. If you were bright and cute and fun, the guys wanted to go out with you. They knew

I wasn't one of the wild and crazy free spirits. I was very serious about my education.

In my junior year I decided to prepare for a career in fashion. I spent my summers selling at Gertrude Herron's boutique in Auburn and loved the work. I knew this would be my career after graduation. When Bonwit Teller in New York requested one student from twelve Eastern colleges be selected to represent their school in a new College Shop concept they were initiating, I immediately applied. It was scheduled for summer vacation between junior and senior year.

W.S.G.A. Student government leaders at Cornell. I am in the back row, first on the right.

All expenses would be paid for travel, but we would be responsible for our own place to live for six weeks. I was very excited when I was interviewed and finally selected to go to New York representing Cornell. I guess I convinced the school I was seriously interested in a fashion career. What a wonderful opportunity! The farthest I'd traveled at that point was to Syracuse and Ithaca, so it was really an adventure and the true beginning of my career in fashion.

I arrived the middle of July and left the end of August. My first impression of the city was written in my diary: "Boy! was I excited about New York. There's just too much of it, that's all. My little room 322 here at the Central Club for Nurses isn't the most elegant place in the world and even at two dollars nightly I thought I was being robbed!" The room was very small and painted a drab off-white. There was a single bed, a chair, and a small table. The bathroom was at the end of the hall. I stayed there for one week until I arranged to share an apartment with one of the girls in the College Shop for the balance of my time in New York.

At Bonwit Teller, we were trained and assigned different departments until the College Shop opened on the fifth floor. We were there to sell! From the beginning, I loved the store and the quality of its merchandise and clientele. One day I was helping a leading actress on Broadway and the next day a Hollywood star! Gloria de Haven was one of my celebrities. She was starring on Broadway at the time. I sold her some deep lavender velvet separates that were featured in the store windows that week. She particularly liked the fuller pants and the tight, short jacket. I talked her into buying the skirt also. "You can't wear pants to a lot of places," I commented. She agreed and bought it without hesitating.

I was totally swept up by the glamour of it all, even though there were plenty of ordinary days as well. On Sundays and days off, I wanted to "see it all," and became the supreme tourist. Uptown, downtown, mid-town, East Side, West Side, North Side, South Side, the Metropolitan Museum, the Cloisters, the Village, Grand Central Station, the antique shops on Third Avenue, Central Park, Macy's, Gimbels, and an occasional glimpse at night spots like the Stork Club or afternoon tea at the Plaza were a few of the highlights I visited more than once. It was a hot summer in New York, but I was determined and walked everywhere. The city was much safer in the fifties and sixties, and I never worried when I was out alone at night. Memories of those six weeks convinced me that after graduation, retailing would be my career and New York City would be my home. It was the only field I was interested in and the only city I wanted to live in.

I returned to Cornell to complete my senior year. Reminiscing about my first three years at school reminds me of the really nice men who played a part in my life at that time. Bob Smith was a steady throughout my sophomore year. He was really sweet and kind, and I wore his fraternity pin for a year. Dick Reid and I were really good friends and dated for about a year also. There were many very interesting men at Cornell, including Kapur, a young student from India who was brilliant and a little mysterious. In junior year, however, my big college sweetheart came along and everyone else fell by the wayside. Ken Battles and I had the longest relationship

Cornell had plenty of men to date. Here I am with Bob Smith in sophomore year.

With Dick Reid in sophomore/junior years

of them all. We really "fell in love," which led to my meeting his parents in Massachusetts and receiving an engagement ring. I thought we'd be married after my graduation, but something happened during that trip that made me realize I didn't want to be tied down. On my last day there I quietly asked Ken to have breakfast away from his home so that we could talk privately. We went to a neighborhood coffee shop, and I could sense Ken was curious and nervous as though he sensed something was wrong.

"What's up, honey? What's going on?" he asked quietly.

I looked at him directly and just blurted it out. "Ken, I can't keep your ring. It was a total surprise when you gave it to me, and I wasn't prepared. You have just graduated from Cornell, and I have one more year to go. I'd like my independence and a career in New York when I graduate, not marriage and children. Here's your beautiful ring back, and I hope you understand it's not you, it's me."

I was almost ready to cry as I looked at Ken. He was slumped in his coffee shop chair, one arm resting on the table and the other on the back of the chair. He was shocked. His handsome face was looking down at the table. He pulled himself up and leaned

Ken Battles and me in junior year

forward, arms folded in front of him, and looked me in the eyes. "What a surprise. Why did you wait until the last minute? Are you sure this is what you want?" He was hurting.

"I'm sure, and I'm so sorry this happened. I can't help it. It's over." I was relieved to say it.

The rest of my senior year flew by. During that time, there was a competition sponsored by Revlon to select the girl who would represent Cornell as "Miss Fashion Plate." Many of us entered, and much to my surprise, I won. There was plenty of press coverage and I received a year's supply of Revlon cosmetics. Uppermost in my mind, however, was graduation and my return to Bonwit Teller. They had already contacted me, and I was to begin work the end of June. I was happy they hadn't forgotten me! When graduation day finally arrived, it was the long awaited fulfillment of my mother's and my dreams. She came to the graduation exercises with my sister, Helen, driving down from Auburn to Ithaca for the last time.

When I later found them in the crowd, my mother put her arms around me and tearfully said, " I am very, very proud of you, Olga. Your college education is my gift to you."

I looked at this kind, sweet, roly-poly woman who worked in the rope company to save money for my college expenses and I wanted to cry. "Thank you, Mama, for making it possible for me to go to Cornell!" I have never forgotten that moment, nor the unspoken belief and love my mother had for me. She asked for nothing, only that I DO it, because she knew I was intelligent and capable and headed for success. She was so proud of me, her college graduate daughter.

Olga Myslichuk, Class of 1950

FOUR

Manhattan

First Job in Fashion

NEW YORK CITY, HERE I COME! It was 1950 and I was thrilled to have a job instead of looking for one. But I did need to find an apartment that I could afford. Two of my Cornell classmates and I decided to look for something we could share. We were temporarily staying at the "Y" in a tiny, bleak room, because we soon realized how expensive it was to live in the nicer parts of town. We decided to rent a fourth floor walk-up on West 49th Street in the midst of Hell's Kitchen. Location bad. Rent good. My salary at the time was twenty-eight dollars a week, but I managed on a strict budget of eating at home or in cafeterias. The three of us were pretty compatible. Two of us slept in the bedroom and one on the couch. Last one in from a date was required to sleep on the couch. Alone.

" I'll meet you at the bottom of the stairs," was our usual greeting to our dates.

"No sense in your coming all the way up those stairs, just to go all the way down," was our standard good night.

If we really liked someone and wanted a good necking session, we wouldn't say anything. We would trudge upstairs together and take over the beaten up couch for a few hours. It wasn't the best of arrangements, so needless to say, we didn't live there very long.

My first job at Bonwit Teller was head-of-stock in sportswear on the seventh floor. I really liked it and soon learned how to manage the department from the buyer. She was very demanding and ordered me never, NEVER, to leave any merchandise hanging in the stock room unless it had a reason for being there. Head-of-stock is one notch higher than salesgirl. I was responsible for all the inventory, displays, transfers, alterations, special orders, appearance of the department and stockroom, fill-in requests from the salesgirls, on and on.

Several months later, management decided I should have a more diversified experience and transferred me to the main floor glove department. Yuk! I made instant friends with Bridie, the top sales-girl, who loved, loved, loved gloves. She taught me how to prop-erly put on those soft leather gloves and explained the difference between six button, eight button, and sixteen button length gloves. She liked me because I was eager to learn, but for some strange rea-son the glove buyer took an instant dislike to me. This was a new experience and I wasn't sure what to do. I decided to simply do my best. I came in early, windexed the glass cases, asked questions, and sold plenty of gloves; I hoped she would notice and approve and learn to like me. Instead, she was frigid around me and detached. It was as though I didn't exist. I was in the glove department for a total of about three weeks and wished management would transfer me to ready-to-wear. I was very excited when, a few days later, I was called up to personnel. "Maybe this will give me a chance to talk about a transfer," I thought. Imagine my surprise when I sat down and the personnel director immediately informed me, "Ollie, I'm sorry to tell you this but management has decided to let you go." That was it. "But why?" I asked. I was really shocked. She said something about not having anything further to discuss, so I quietly gathered up my belongings in my locker and left, feeling like a failure. As I walked up Fifth Avenue, all I could think about was, "What did I do?" "Why didn't they tell me?" "Where do I go now?" The more I thought about it the more unfair it became. "I'll show them! Someday they'll be sorry they lost me!"

My salary lasted from week to week, so I had to find employment quickly. I went back to the apartment, walked listlessly up the end-less stairs, entered the gloomy rooms, and had a good cry. Then I pulled out my typewriter and decided to write a glowing resume.

That same afternoon I called several Fifth Avenue stores requesting appointments, including Saks Fifth Avenue, Lord and Taylor, and DePinna. I wanted to work on Fifth Avenue! I was going to call Bloomingdales if nothing happened with these three, but much to my surprise, each store made time for me that week . DePinna called first. I went there the following day and met with John Fielder, the president, and Ed Hoffman, the merchandise manager. It was a long interview, and I was my usual enthusiastic, perky self. They had an opening for a buyer of coats, suits, and dresses.

"With no buying experience, do you think you can do the job?" Ed Hoffman asked.

My quick reply was, "I learn quickly, and if you take me around the market and guide me on the initial Buy, I'm sure I can."

I wanted that job! They said they would let me know the following day. I was thrilled to think I might be a BUYER!!! It was a long evening. The following morning I was called in for a follow-up interview with Ed Hoffman.

He told me, "I'm willing to take a chance on you, but Mr. Fielder is reluctant. He doesn't think someone as attractive as you could possibly be smart enough. I disagree, and since he's authorized me to make the decision, I'm offering you the position."

Bells began to ring! My heart pounded. "You will never be sorry," I said. He never was.

This was a perfect example of being in the right place at the right time, because when I walked into DePinna that morning they had been looking for a buyer. Ed Hoffman told me, many months later, he had a gut feeling about me immediately and could see by my appearance that I had the kind of taste the store needed. He spent many hours early on personally training me, reviewing and revising budgets, and introducing me to the market on Seventh Avenue. At that time DePinna was considered a "little old lady" store, having established its reputation with stodgy, average-looking clothes. Transforming that image was not going to be easy. The change would be gradual, because we didn't want to lose the existing clientele while attracting the new. Little by little the look of the floor began to sparkle. The clothes were younger, more colorful, and up-to-date. I bought coats, suits, and dresses and coordinated them into color groups. Displays were grouped with many mannequins instead of just one floating here and another there. Fifth Avenue windows were given to us on a regular basis and brought many new customers into the store. The challenge to build the volume came next, and projections had to be realistic. Ed Hoffman and I spent a great deal of time together in the "market" that first year. He recognized immediately what I was trying to do.

One day he called me to his office and cautioned me, "Ollie, I hope you're not trying to make DePinna too sophisticated and fashionable too quickly. It might scare the customers away. I, personally, love what you are doing and support you one hundred percent. But it takes time."

"Don't worry, Mr. Hoffman, the vendors are with us and have committed to helping us if we can't sell fashion. But I really believe we can and I'm determined to stay this course. Just let me buy the way I see it and I promise you in one year we will double our figures."

"Okay, Miss Ollie, I'll leave it up to you. You've certainly got everyone in the market talking about what's happening at DePinna, and it's all good. They say how easy you are to work with, that you're decisive and pleasant, and you don't waste any time. You're obviously well-liked."

Retailing came naturally to me, and I loved every ten-hour day I spent in the store. Mr Hoffman was very attractive, charming, and enthusiastic about the incredible changes taking place in the department. He was very enthusiastic about me too. He would visit us several times a day to see how we were doing and tell us how wonderful we all were. And sure enough, about a year later, every figure in the department had more than doubled. He was very proud of us and made a point of telling the staff how he felt. It was, after all, a team effort.

"The art of buying and selling clothes is instinctive with Miss Ollie," he said. "Ending up with a sizeable profit her first year is a remarkable accomplishment in itself, but gradually changing the look of the department through her impeccable taste has been a thrill for management to watch. Her figures speak for themselves. We are very proud of you, Miss Ollie, and look forward to another year of growth together."

All I could say was, "Thank you for believing in me. It never would have happened if you hadn't taken a chance on an inexperienced but enthusiastic twenty-two year old. How could I have let you down."

We had a close, warm relationship, but since he was married it never went very far. By this time I was living in Tudor City in a one room apartment on an upper floor with a spectacular view overlooking the East River. I could see the 59th Street bridge with unending traffic, tug boats pulling cargo, and the magical transformation at night when city lights came on. My bed folded up into the wall, and it was a pain every night to pull it down and every morning pull it up. But the view was worth it. I lived there for about two years, a definite improvement over the Hell's Kitchen apartment. But things were about to change.

I was happy at DePinna until Ed Hoffman accepted another much bigger position with a store in the Midwest. After he left, I received a call from Jay Rossbach who was a merchandise manager at Saks Fifth Avenue. I'd been at DePinna about two years.

"We hear very good things about you, Ollie, especially from our vendors in the market. They tell me you're an excellent buyer and helped turn Depinna around with a new image. Your selections turn out to be best sellers, and you are well liked by the people with whom you work. We would like to talk to you. Can you come by in the next day or two?"

We set up an appointment for the following day. The current buyer, Grace Buchanan, was leaving and they needed an immediate replacement. I had met her in the market and had spoken to her on several occasions. Mr. Rossbach told me I was the only person she had recommended for the position and after talking to some key vendors about me he wanted to meet me. The following day I walked into Saks Fifth Avenue and couldn't believe I might be working there before the day was over. I took the elevator to the eighth floor where the executive officers were and walked to Jay

Rossbach's office. As I entered, he stood up at his desk and held out his hand. He was very tall, well dressed, and quite tan from a recent vacation.

In a booming voice I would get to know so well, he greeted me. "So you're the Miss Ollie I've been hearing so much about! I'm happy to finally meet you."

"Thank you, Mr. Rossbach. I'm happy to meet you too. I've seen you here and there in the market at some of the shows. Saks always gets the best seats in the house." (What a dumb thing to say, I instantly thought.)

He chuckled and continued, "I wanted to know more about you before we met so I made a few phone calls to our vendors. Both Anne and Ben Klein from Jr. Sophisticates said you were the best thing that ever happened to DePinna. You were smart and had great taste. Mr. Kalish over at Arkay said you should be with Saks because you were headed 'for the big time.' Everyone I spoke to had glowing remarks. Now that I've met you, I can appreciate their enthusiasm. Tell me, Ollie, how would you like to join us here at Saks?"

Just like that I was offered the biggest buyer's position in the field, with twenty stores to buy for and a volume in the millions. "I'd love it," I replied with an I-can-hardly-believe-this-is-happening voice, "but I'll have to give at least two week's notice to DePinna to find a replacement for me. I'll be in your office as soon as I can.

When I told Mr. Fielder I was leaving DePinna to join Saks Fifth Avenue, he was very happy for me but sorry to lose me. As it turned out, my assistant was offered the job, and since she was already familiar with the department I was able to leave within a few days. Little did I know the next decade would bring about some of the most interesting experiences of my life!

I *loved* my job from the moment I started! My office was located on the seventh floor overlooking Fifth Avenue directly across from Rockefeller Plaza. Every day I looked down at the sculpture of "Atlas Struggling to Lift Planet Earth" in the entry courtyard of Rockefeller Center. I looked down at the crowds walking up and down Fifth Avenue, enjoying the excitement and pace of the city. I loved the change of seasonal flowers in the huge flower beds in the courtyard and the annual raising of the tallest Christmas tree at the other end by the skating rink. Every St. Patrick's Day, we had the best view of the annual parade that went on and on for hours down Fifth Avenue. It was an exciting time to feel and touch and be part of the New York Scene.

I started my new job going into the market with Miss Buchanan. She introduced me to our most important vendors, and after several days of intensive training, she was ready to leave and have me take over. I couldn't wait! It was the beginning of my serious worka-holic habits, all consuming and single-purposed. I was determined to succeed, though it never occurred to me I wouldn't. From the beginning, days were never long enough. I used to go to daily Mass at St. Patrick's right across the street from our employee entrance on Fiftieth Street. My days started early and ended about seven. I usually had my arms full of journals and out-of-town reports as I walked home to Tudor City. Every night I studied to familiar-ize myself with the department in New York as well as all twenty branch stores. Several months later management decided it was time I visit the biggest of the out-of-town stores in Chicago, Beverly Hills, Detroit, San Francisco, etc. I was thrilled to go, not only to see the stores but to visit these cities for the first time.

When summer vacation came, I decided to travel to Europe for three weeks. I was in my mid- twenties and had never been out of the country before. I wanted to see Paris, Rome, and Florence. One of my male friends gave me the name of Paul de Ganay to look up in Paris. "Don't be intimidated by Paul," my friend warned me, "He's very handsome and comes from a distinguished family. I'll call Paris and let him know the dates you'll be there."

"Great!" I thought to myself, "I didn't know anyone in Paris and this sounded interesting."

When I arrived in France for the first part of my journey, I was grateful I'd studied French for four years in high school. Much of it came back as I began to use the language. My first encounter was with the taxicab driver. My French was obviously too bro-ken for him. To this day I'm certain my tip was as big as the cab ride. "*Combien?*" I kept asking him. He insisted some outrageous amount and I kept repeating, *"Tres beaucoup,"* *"Tres beaucoup."* I had no choice but to pay him. I was in Paris! And nothing was going to spoil my trip.

I couldn't wait to walk in the streets, even though jet lag was beginning to take over. I left my bags packed and went out in the balmy French air. I couldn't believe I was in Paris, me, the little small town girl from upstate New York was in Paris! After about an hour I returned to the hotel, exhausted from the trip, the walk, the anticipation, and the reality, I lay on the bed and instantly fell into a deep sleep. Since New York-to-Paris flights arrived in Paris early in the morning, I slept all day and into the night, awakening about midnight. It took a few days to get into the Paris rhythm. When I was back to normal, I called Paul de Ganay and chatted for a few minutes. We made plans to meet for lunch the following day. He suggested a little restaurant around the corner that would be easy for me to find. When we finally met the next day, I was delighted to find him not only handsome, but charming and interesting. It was a long lunch, and when we were almost ready to leave he mentioned he was driving to the South of France the following day for about a week. Would I like to go with him? He had his boat in Cannes and was planning to make a few stops during his stay.

"I would love to, but I want to see more of Paris while I'm here. I only have three more days before leaving for Rome."

"Oh, Ollie," he said, "Rome is just a big city that is very hot in the summer. Change your plans! Come with me!"

He was very persuasive. By the time we finished lunch, it was decided I would fly down after my three days in Paris and call him when I arrived. I had to do some fast changes in my itinerary. The only problem was giving up three of six days planned for Rome. I might not be able to get another room because of peak tourist season, but I decided to take my chances. I arrived in Cannes three days later, called Paul on the boat, and spent three glorious days with him and his boat full of beautiful people. The women were all dressed in Pucci bikinis and pareros, bright prints and lots of body showing. They were all French or Italian and very attractive. I was the only American aboard, and with my All-American Girl classic pants and shirts I was reluctant to put on my Esther Williams one piece bathing suit that suddenly made me feel frumpy and dated. I was introduced to Party-Party-French style. Couples, not necessarily together, would periodically wander downstairs and "do it." I didn't catch on until I noticed Paul with one gorgeous creature go down and return about a half hour later. He came over to me a little later and easily led me by the hand downstairs. When he took both hands and slowly lowered the top of my bathing suit, I panicked. Mortal sin lurking. I quickly ran around him and upstairs. What should I do?

Paul came up a few minutes later, this handsome, 6′1″, tan Adonis, and sweetly asked, "Would you like some white wine or a glass of Perrier?"

My memory of those few days was pleasant enough, but Paul played kneesies with any pretty little thing sitting next to him. I soon realized it was one communal playground, and I hadn't learned how to play the game. It reminded me of a French version of Cornell house parties.

At the end of three, short, glorious days sailing the beautiful Mediterranean, with a memorable stop in St. Tropez, I packed my bags and flew to Rome. When I arrived at the hotel they informed me there wasn't a single room left! I was

My memorable stop in St. Tropez

afraid that might happen, but it was my lucky day. Standing at the opposite end of the desk was a familiar business friend, Freddie Pomerantz. He very gallantly instructed the concierge to give me one of the reserved rooms in his suite. I must have looked a little apprehensive but he immediately explained that he always reserved two or three additional rooms for buyers who didn't realize how difficult it was to get rooms in peak season. He was one of my important vendors and at that moment was a walking guardian angel. I thanked him very much, and was doubly grateful when I saw the lavish quarters he so kindly gave to me. Rome was exciting and full of history, and, yes, the weather was hot! I took every tour I had time for in three days. Freddie and his entourage took me under their wings, and we wined and dined and shook the rooms each evening with boisterous laughter. I wished I had more time to stay, but my next stop turned into my favorite five days of the entire trip.

Taking the train from Rome to Florence for the first time was an adventure. The train station was so crowded with people, it was difficult to maneuver bags and impossible to find porters to help. Finally settled and on our way, I sat in a semi-private area with four Italian men who spoke not one word of English. I carried my English-Italian dictionary everywhere and managed to communicate a little with them. The one thing you notice right away in Italy is the flirtatiousness of the young men. Walking up the streets in Rome, listening to their "ahhhh, bella, bellas," turned me into Sophia Loren right then and there. With my head held high, and my stride a little softer, I responded with a big smile and some innocent body language. By the time my train arrived in Florence, all four men insisted on helping me with my luggage and finding a taxi. I was so happy I threw them four kisses. They, in turn, did the same to me.

After a speedy trip down the narrow, ancient Florentine streets, we arrived at my tiny hotel overlooking the Arno River. Again I left my bags packed. I was so anxious to see this little city full of history, I ran out and started walking and walking. I decided to have lunch, and after eating a little pasta and salad I continued my exploring. The city closes down in the afternoon, so I returned to my hotel, convinced that the best way to see Florence and not miss anything was to go on tours. For five days I went on different tours in and around Florence. In the evenings I found little restaurants and ate what they recommended, convinced "you can't get a bad meal in Italy." I particularly loved this medieval town, because there was so much art, so many works-of-art buildings, so many ancient churches that it was almost impossible to comprehend the enormity of its beauty. I was totally smitten by Florence at first sight and to this day it remains my favorite place in Europe. Little did I know at the time that just a short distance from Florence was the town of St. Gimingnano, the inspiration for our store, CAPRICCIO, at the Borgata in Scottsdale, Arizona, which was built twenty years later.

I was sad to go. It was like leaving another world. My vacation was over, and I needed to take the train from Florence to Milan to catch my flight back to New York. I slept most of the trip back, and when I finally reached my little one-room apartment at Tudor City I was happy to be home. I reminisced along the way about the changes that had already happened to me since coming to New York. I had moved three times. After leaving West 49th Street, I lived in the Bronx with Jeanette, a friend I'd met through friends. One disastrous experience in her apartment sent me looking for another place to live. I'd been there only a few days, when one night I awakened and went to the kitchen for a glass of water. When I turned on the light, I was appalled to see every cupboard and shelf covered with huge roaches! The floor, the doors, the ceiling were full of them. I was revolted at the sight and screamed out, "Jeanettttttte, come in here!" She came running in thinking there was someone in the apartment. "Oh, that," she laughed, "aren't they cute?" I just leave them alone and they disappear somewhere in the daytime." I couldn't believe she was saying this. You couldn't step on the floor without squooshing a few of them! They were falling in my hair, and I tried to shake them out. They were crawling up my legs. Ugh! We needed an exterminator now! I stayed a few more days until I found another apartment, and moved out as soon as I did. I never knew what became of the roaches, or Jeanette.

Fortunately, the new apartment was in Manhattan on East 60th Street and didn't require a long subway ride daily. I could walk to work . The girl with whom I was sharing was a college friend, and since I couldn't afford a place of my own yet it would have to do.

Ellen was easy going, and since I hardly knew her it was fascinating to see her in action. She showed me the place, pointing out that the apartment was long and narrow with a hallway turning into a wider hallway and then an alcove with a couch-bed arrangement. At the end was a nice-sized bedroom which Ellen claimed. The alcove was for me. It didn't take long for me to figure out, with her many boyfriends, that she must have been a nymphomaniac. The men paraded in and out, and I, the daily communicant, watched in shock and bewilderment. My roommate was sinning right before my eyes, and I wasn't doing a thing about it. I knew I wouldn't last there very long, so one Sunday surrounded by the New York Times, my coffee, and a toasted English muffin, I confronted her.

"Ellen," I said, "How do you keep track of all these men in your life? I lie there in my cozy couch-bed as you creep down the hallway past me into the bedroom and each night it's a different man!"

"It's fun," she said, "I try to be quiet, but it's dark in the apartment and we occasionally bump into something as we find our way back to my bedroom."

"Did it ever occur to you to ... maybe ... abstain for a few nights?" I boldly asked.

"Ollie, I love men," she replied, "and someone is always there for me."

"Well," I replied, "this arrangement is not going to work for me, and I'll start looking for another place tomorrow." And I did.

I moved into a studio apartment in Tudor City within walking distance of the East River. Finally: solitariness. I didn't even mind the bed in the wall. There was a little kitchenette on one side, a bathroom with a shower, and a comfortable couch with matching chair. There was a round dining table with four chairs that I set up at the window. I enjoyed many candle-lit dinners at that table looking at the variety of boats moving up and down the river. The bridges were lit at night and looked like Christmas garlands. My friends used to tease me by saying you could stand in the middle of the floor and touch all four walls of the apartment. My arms weren't that long. I used to daydream at that window the way I used to as a child overlooking the Kowal's back yard. Here I was doing the same thing, but this time I was in my own little heaven.

Since coming to New York City I had decided to change my name legally from Olga Myslichuk to Ollie Myles. Everyone called me Ollie, and by some quirk I was dubbed Miss Ollie in the market. It stuck and I was Miss Ollie for the rest of my career. My name change helped overcome the perpetual embarrassment of people unable to pronounce my name. While I lived at Tudor City I met

Father Colligan introduced me to my first husband, Judah Holstein

Father Colligan, a young Jesuit priest, who became a close friend. He introduced me to Judah Holstein, a friend of his from San Francisco who, like me, had converted to Catholicism. He was Jewish by birth, and I found his conversion fascinating. We connected immediately on a spiritual level, and by the time he left a week later we were certain our relationship was a pre-ordained "God Thing." Judah was in the army, on his way to basic training camp, when he came to New York to visit Father Colligan. We wrote to each other every day, mostly about spiritual stuff and our feelings. I was fascinated by his ability to analyze the lives of his favorite saints, explain commitment, and why he, a young Jewish man, decided to become a Catholic. He attended daily mass and received communion. He wasn't like anyone I'd ever met before. He visited me in New York twice before he was shipped to Korea and was given a week off before going. By this time we had known each other about eight months. We must have exchanged more than a hundred letters.

Father Colligan kept track of our relationship and said several times, "Judah is the right man for you, Ollie. Why don't you two get married before he goes overseas."

It hadn't occurred to me until he kept insisting I think about it seriously. When Judah asked me to marry him during a phone call, I thought, "Is this meant to be? Has Father Colligan been talking to him about this?"

Once again I felt like I was being swept up in a current and couldn't get out. Work was my refuge, but work also blinded me to being swept up by the wrong man. I wasn't really sure how I felt about marriage and didn't know why I said, "Yes," but honestly felt that God was watching over me and this was what He wanted. How immature and inexperienced I was! Thinking back on it today, I still can't explain the foolishness of that decision.

Judah Holstein with my mother

A few weeks later we were married in the Catholic church. Judah was given a week off before being shipped to Korea, and we had a few days for our honeymoon. It turned out to be a disaster. We were both sexually inexperienced, and since I was still a virgin it was not a pleasant first encounter. He tried and tried until I finally had to give up and say, "Stop, it just hurts too much." We tried again the following day with the same results. We left the third day without consummating the marriage. He went to Korea and I went back to my job as though nothing had ever happened. But something had happened. I was living exactly as before. He hadn't moved in, and I was no longer the independent, single girl. In the beginning we wrote many letters, but after a few weeks the letters were fewer and shorter. I found myself resenting the position I was in. I knew in my heart I had made a mistake, and as the year overseas dragged on, I decided the marriage was a pathetic reality and needed to be ended.

When Judah returned from Korea, I flew to San Francisco to meet him and also his mother . By now I couldn't face being alone with this stranger-husband. I had built such a giant resentment against him, I was confused, unhappy, and ready to explode. Our original plan was to drive back to New York from San Francisco. Judah wanted to return to New York to live, so we decided to "get to know each other" again. Perhaps there was still a spark left in the relationship. Judah insisted he still loved me very much and tried to be understanding about my mixed-up feelings. It was so hard. We left after a few days and faced the long automobile trip back to New York like two strangers confined together in a small, self-imposed, moving prison cell. Our nightly stops were the worst. I couldn't stand having him touch me! We ended each evening the same way, he was angry and hurt and I was incapable of responding to him. We finally had a long talk about everything that was on my mind. I no longer loved him and I wanted a divorce. It was that simple. He couldn't understand what had happened over that one year, and I wasn't able to explain it.

The remainder of the trip was filled with endless silence followed by frustrated blowups. I dreaded our arrival in New York City, because he made it clear he intended to live in my apartment until he found a job. Fortunately, I had rented a larger apartment in Tudor City several months earlier. We decided he could temporarily sleep on the couch in the living room and I would have my bedroom. Each morning I left early for work and returned each evening to find him still on the couch in his pajamas. He lay on the couch most of the day, every day. I, meanwhile, went to St. Patrick's rectory to talk to the priest regarding an annulment or a divorce. It all seemed so complicated because the church didn't recognize divorce except for certain conditions. Judah left it up to me, and before long he decided it was time to go. He packed his bags and was gone, only to leave me with the promise he wouldn't contest the divorce and to send him the papers for his signature. It was impossible to do anything with the church, so I was advised to fly to Mexico and obtain a valid "Mexican divorce." I returned with my own name once again. I heard from Judah and Father Colligan a few times, but it wasn't long before I learned Judah had decided to move back to the California. I never heard from him again.

FIVE

Welcome to Saks Fifth Avenue

My Career as a Buyer

At Saks Fifth Avenue, I was very busy; our sales figures had doubled in the past three years. I was thrilled when, one day, I was called up to the president's office. Going to Adam Gimbel's office was a big deal, and this was the first time for me.

"Sit down, Ollie," he said. "I want to personally congratulate you on the outstanding results in your department. You not only had the biggest increase in volume in the store last year, but you also had the most profitable. I would like to use your department as an example to others of what can be accomplished. How did you do it?"

We talked for almost an hour. I'll never forget it. "Looking back is easy," I smiled. "Looking ahead is the challenge." I shared with him the importance of controlling inventories in all the stores, staying within budget, taking timely markdowns, and when to reorder. A week later, at the annual buyer's meeting, I was singled out and my department's figures were reviewed. For the next few weeks I was flattered by the many buyers who called or came by my office to congratulate me. Some even asked for help, particularly on how to reduce their markdowns. I would always say the same thing. "Don't overbuy. Don't reorder too late. Control your inventories."

Though the work load was enormous, I had a bright new assistant, Cathy Sotir. She had graduated from the University of Michigan and was a leader on campus, achieving high honors and a long

I met Cathy (Sotir) Apothaker at Saks Fifth Avenue. We became lifelong friends.

list of extracurricular activities. She was only about five feet two inches tall with thick brunette hair and a tendency to put on weight. She was well-spoken and bright. I spotted her the day she was made manager of the seventh floor where my department was located. After a month or two, I finally asked management to promote her to my assistant buyer. The timing was right, and Jay Rossbach, my merchandise manager, approved the promotion. Cathy and I had a lot in common. Her parents were Greek immigrants, and she experienced some of the same feelings I had growing up: shame, lack of approval, and little communication with her parents.

Soon we were comparing stories and became good friends. One evening she invited me to her apartment for dinner and greeted me wearing one of her signature loose black dresses that always reminded me of monastic minimalism. No jewelry; just plain black. No makeup; just her own smooth olive complexion and beautiful big Greek eyes. She served us peanut butter and jelly sandwiches with a glass of milk. I couldn't stop laughing.

"What's a nice Greek girl like you doing serving peanut butter sandwiches and milk for dinner!" I blurted.

"I never learned how to cook," she said. "I live on peanut butter and jelly sandwiches."

"That's hard to believe," I told her, "but from now on I'm taking you out to dinner or we're eating at my place."

My place was now a beautiful one-room apartment at 60 Sutton Place South. I had moved from Tudor City, and for the first time decided to rent unfurnished. I was going to buy my own furniture this time. I didn't want to make any disastrous mistakes, so I hired a decorator from William Pahlmann. I had so much to learn, and the Pahlmann firm came highly recommended. It was my first experience working with a decorator, and I soon realized how exciting it could be to see empty space transformed before my eyes. "I want everything creamy beige," I told him, "walls, couches, chairs, rugs, draperies." We selected fabrics together and placed our orders. Then came the inevitable wait. It took about six months before everything was ready, but the end result was incredibly creamy beige-beautiful. I still remember the deeply piled v'Soske rug, pale and plush, awaiting the arrival of the furniture to be placed like so many objects in a painting and transforming the space into something beautiful.

As we completed the apartment and I slept in it for the first time, I felt I had passed a rite of passage. It was five years earlier in 1950 that I was living in Hell's Kitchen on West forty-ninth Street, earning twenty-eight dollars a week, and sharing a fourth floor walk-up with two other girls. I

Many weekends we would take these orphan children to the park to play

had so much to be grateful for, most of all my job at Saks Fifth Avenue. I had been with the store for little over three years, but so much had happened in such a short time. I had moved three times, held two different jobs, and was married and divorced. Finally, my life was coming together.

Official portrait of me as "Safinia" of Saks Fifth Avenue

Thoughts of my mother kept returning for about a year. How I regretted not seeing more of her when she was alive! How I loved to hear her laugh and see her eyes twinkle! How I appreciated her home-cooking! How grateful I was for her contribution to my college education! How sad it was she was killed so young. Eventually it eased up and I found myself once again totally immersed in work.

Management decided we should develop an exclusive label in my department, and we came up with the name SAFINIA. The SFA in SaFiniA represented Saks Fifth Avenue. "Ollie, how do you see this developing into a regular collection? What vendors should we use? How often should we do this? How many styles should we develop?" Jay Rossbach asked.

I was thrilled with the whole idea and replied, "Let me think about this for a few days and I'll get back to you."

As a buyer for Saks Fifth Avenue, I was required to buy for all twenty stores in the chain. (Today, there are many more.) It was important that their inventories stay on budget, with new merchandise arriving regularly and old stock marked down or returned to New York. I planned my own budgets annually for all the stores. My taste level for a high fashion store like Saks was very important, because we catered to a wealthier client who looked to us for simple,

Publicity photograph of me in a "Safinia" dress   *Publicity photograph of me in a "Safinia" coat*

elegant, exciting clothes. My department was on the seventh floor, and we carried all the good designers. Everybody wanted to sell Saks Fifth Avenue. Developing this new Safinia line was exactly what we were looking for.

At that time there was a big need for more sophisticated styling and better quality fabrics, but the market was afraid of higher prices. I assured them our orders would support the shift. I talked to a few of my most important vendors, discussing exclusivity in all our cities on the styles we would work out together. That meant no other store where there were Saks stores could carry the collection. I spent hours with various designers selecting styles and discussing the look we wanted to achieve for our introductory line. We would limit the collection to twenty styles, use European fabrics, and concentrate on design simplicity. My department carried sizes seven through fifteen, (equivalent to sizes six through sixteen). I asked my vendors to develop sizes three and five for the Safinia Collection, because we had so many petite clients. At first they were reluctant, but they all agreed, and eventually we attracted many smaller women who became some of our best size three and five Safinia customers. We developed the collection into the most important group promoted in our area of the store. There were four groups a year; two major ones in the Spring and Fall and two lesser ones for summer and winter. The styling made it a huge success, because we focused on simplicity and beautiful fabrics. It was young couture without the high price tag. The store promoted the collection with full page *New York Times* ads and beautiful windows. I became Safinia and did personal appearances in all the major stores. Mannequins were made to my likeness and used in all Safinia windows, as were photographs of me in all the ads. It personalized the collection, and gave our department something special and exclusive.

While all of this was happening at the store, I was living the "single, career girl" life outside. I had put my short marriage behind me and resolved that in future relationships I would be more careful. There were some interesting men, but no one special. On one trip to the Palm Beach Saks Fifth Avenue store, I decided to take a two-week vacation and stay at the Colony Hotel. I was used to traveling alone, and after two days at the store I was ready to take it easy. The following morning I went out on the deck to sunbathe, and for the first time in months felt totally relaxed. As I slowly luxuriated in the warmth of the Palm Beach air, I sensed a shadow over part of my body. I opened my eyes and looked up. Standing there was a very handsome stranger who looked vaguely familiar.

"Are you alone?" he asked, "And if so, may I join you?"

"Yes. I'm alone. Please join me." I replied. "I've been relaxing here on this glorious morning trying to catch a little sunshine. Is it possible we've met before? You look vaguely familiar."

"I don't believe so," he said extending his hand to shake mine. "I'm John Newland. It's awfully lonely sitting there by myself."

"And I'm Ollie Myles," I responded. "It's nice to see a friendly face."

We chatted for a few minutes and I suddenly remembered he was an actor I'd seen many times on television. We talked about his work, my work, and ordered lunch. While we were eating, he asked me what my plans were for the next few days.

"I have no plans except to spend a week or so here and possibly fly over to Havana after that," I told him happily.

Glamour Magazine did an article on me with a full-page portrait...

"Good!" he replied, "Then you don't have to change any plans. I thought I might drive down to Fort Lauderdale for a few days, then to Miami, and return here at the end of the week. Please come with me."

*Small-city girl;
Miss Ollie
grew up in
quiet Auburn, N. Y.*

*Big-city career: Now her life
centers around Manhattan; her
office is across the street from
sky-scraping Rockefeller Center*

Her career is her taste

Ollie Myles—small, neatly curved brunette with ivory skin and Siamese-cat-blue eyes—
has the dreamy 9-to-5 job of buying beautiful clothes. As buyer of Better Junior Dresses
for Saks Fifth Avenue, New York, she's her own best model; admits, "Shopping for my
department is like shopping for myself and my friends. I'm inclined to buy only clothes
I like." Fortunately, her taste in clothes is tempting to hundreds of young New Yorkers
who count on her department to have what's hot off the fashion griddle. Each season
"Miss Ollie" has a special collection of "Safinia" clothes. She explains, "Safinia is not
just a store name on a label; to me she's a real, rather hard-to-please personality.
Any dress I choose for the Safinia collection has to live up to her tastes." Here, in a
capsule are Safinia's (or Miss Ollie's) fashion demands: she likes up-to-the-minute
fashions, isn't afraid of extreme silhouettes, *e.g.*, this year's chemise; loves pleats,
steers clear of skirts that are bunchy at the waist; likes black for daytime, bright
colors for evening; hates ruffles; loves textured fabrics. *(Continued on the next page)*

9 *o'clock—as buyer
for Saks Fifth Avenue's
Better Junior Dresses—
Miss Ollie looks polished
and precise, usually*
*wears a handsome black dress.
Left, in the stock room she ruffles
through a shipment of party dresses.
Right, she does paper work
in her tiny, sun-lit office.
Below, she checks orders
with her two assistants.*

DE MORGOLI

SANTE FORLAND

5 *o'clock—at home Miss Ollie relaxes
from a fast-paced day ... wears
bright colors, full-skirted dresses.
Above: full-length at-home dress
in bright-red plaid cotton.*

73

,,,and a two-page story on my career

Miss Ollie *continued*

*Dressing table, left, reveals
that Miss Ollie loves perfume,
is mad for pearls . . . wears
them with everything.
Below, in her beautiful,
under-played living room.
Color scheme—shades of beige,
off-white, and gold.*

After hours, Miss Ollie's fashion personality changes from a handsome, understated look to one that's bright and striking. Entertaining in her beige-and-gold apartment? She's likely to wear a bright-colored, long at-home costume. For informal dates? She has two straight-hanging chemise dresses (says 95% of the men she meets like them)—one is red wool jersey, one bright pink flannel. For a cocktail party? Bare-backed sheath in bright navy faille. Miss Ollie has strong ideas about accessories: She likes rather roomy, neat leather purses, plain pointed pumps with very high heels (these and her high-topped coiffure make her look taller than her 5′ 5″). Her jewelry weakness is pearls. She has six pairs of earrings—all variations of the pearl button; and several fake-pearl necklaces, most of them ropes. She says, "Dazzling costume jewelry looks fine on other women . . . never feels right on me. I try to get rich effects with jewel colors, plushy fabrics." (If you're a Miss Ollie type, it works.)

7 *o'clock*

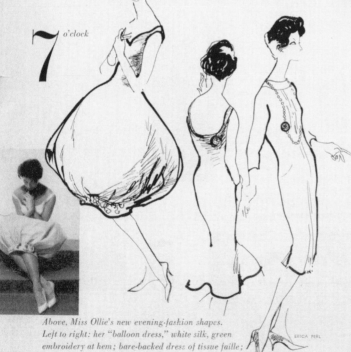

*Above, Miss Ollie's new evening-fashion shapes.
Left to right: her "balloon dress," white silk, green
embroidery at hem; bare-backed dress of tissue faille;
chemise of shock-pink tissue flannel.*

ERICA PERL

Miss Ollie's choice of white... for holidays and resort

Beginning opposite, a preview of Miss Ollie's
new "Safinia" collection of white
party dresses, worn by GLAMOUR models.
Opposite page, left: White silk one-piece
shift. (Miss Ollie says, "I'm sold
on this fitted 'unfitted look'...
it suggests a nice figure underneath.")
By Jerry Greenwald in linen-like silk
by Chardon Marche. 5-15. About $40.
Jewelry by Trifari.
Opposite page, right: Dress with overblouse,
Miss Ollie's choice because
"The middy look is important, of course . . .
this outfit is wonderful because under
the middy is a handsome scoop-necked sheath."
By Arkay Jr. in Chardon Marche crepe
of Avisco rayon and Celanese acetate. 5-15.
About $40. "Gold-and-turquoise" jewelry
from Piazza Montici.
Both dresses at: Saks Fifth Avenue, all stores

SANTE FORLANO
GLAMOUR, DECEMBER, 1957

It sounded like fun, and I had nothing holding me back in Palm Beach. We had dinner that evening and left the following morning. What a glorious few days we had, sunning, swimming, driving around, lunching on the beach in Fort Lauderdale, and dancing away each evening. I have always loved to dance, and moving around the dance floor in his arms was pretty heady stuff. I felt like Ginger Rogers! The experience was a first for me because John was so attentive. It wasn't the wine, the food, or the sensuous dancing that made me lose all sense of the former "good little girl." I was smitten by this 6'2", lanky, handsome, meticulously groomed, dressed in perfectly tailored everything, Don Juan. He was special, and when he led me up to my bedroom that first night in Fort Lauderdale, I was ready to fall into his arms. He discovered that I not only didn't have a diaphragm, I didn't even know what one was. He couldn't believe what I was saying; it sounded preposterous to him that a young attractive girl like me was so innocent. When I told him my only sexual encounter had been with my ex-husband, and that I had been a virgin up to that point, he stared at me like I was from some outer world.

"It's true," I said, "I never thought there was anything unusual about it."

He looked at me for a few minutes, put his arms around me, and before I knew what was happening we were both flailing around naked in the bed. He had finally broken my fear and reserve regarding sex.

"Ollie, the first thing you should do when you return to New York is see your doctor and get a diaphragm. Meanwhile, we'll be careful," he said matter-of-factly.

We spent the rest of our time together in harmonious bliss.

A few days later John left Palm Beach for New York, and I decided to fly over to Havana alone. It was a memorable experience; the old Havana of that time was full of life, music, and dancing. I recall one huge dance hall where it was customary for anyone to come up to ask you to dance. It was Cuban music and Cuban dancing. Never have I been so swept off my feet by the rhythm of that music. One dancer in particular kept me busy all evening, and though he was not attractive, his dancing more than made up for it. We did the tango, the rhumba, the samba and swayed and twirled from one set to another. He taught me the real way to dance in Cuba. It was unforgettable. During the daytime, I would go on guided tours or shop in the souvenir markets. Time flew by very quickly, dancing every evening and walking through the streets during the day. I left after four days, flying to Miami and connecting with a flight to New York.

I was back to work with renewed vigor and a deep tan. My assistant, Cathy Sotir, had taken care of the department and reviewed what had happened while I was gone. Business had been good, and we were ready to work on our next Safinia Collection. I suggested to my merchandise manager that I go on an exploratory buying trip to Europe. There was something in the air that kept nudging me about newness, inspiration, and ideas that only Europe could offer. I would buy original samples from Italy and France and adapt them for our collection. These samples gave us inspiration for other styles using details or silhouettes from the original. The fabric might inspire us or the color combination. There were a million ideas to discover while walking down the streets, looking at the windows, watching how the young girls dressed. It was the late fifties, and the European market was not what it was to become ten-twenty years later. There was no Giorgio Armani, Gianni Versace, Karl Lagerfeld. Those designers were just beginning. Jay Rossbach liked the idea of my buying trip, and it was planned for that Spring. Meanwhile, I was scheduled to visit eleven branch stores to do personal appearances with the Safinia Collection. When I returned, Cathy and I did our buying for Early Fall and then I was off to Europe.

Our buying office in Europe made appointments for me in Italy and France. I was assigned to a young Italian girl, Franca Bini, who drove me around to the various showrooms. About the third day, she could see I wasn't responding to the collections because I wasn't taking notes nor was I placing orders. She quizzically asked, "Would you like to see a new young designer no one has heard of that I think has a great deal of talent?"

"That's just what we're looking for," I replied with a hint of excitement in my voice.

"No one from the United States has seen his clothes because he is just beginning. You will be the first buyer to see him," said Franca in a tone of voice that suggested *I have saved the best for last*.

She set up an appointment for the following morning. When we arrived, we were led to a centuries-old marble ballroom, completely empty except for three chairs at one end. I was seated in an antique velvet armchair with Franca next to me.

We were offered coffee, and then the designer appeared and introduced himself, "I am Valentino, and it is with great pleasure I welcome you."

Of course it was spoken in Italian, because he didn't speak a word of English. Franca had to interpret for me. He began the show immediately, one model at a time, wearing brightly colored outfits in lime green, lemon yellow, hot pink, and bright blue. Each one had a matching coat and dress with whimsical turned-back brim hats. (I couldn't resist and at the end of the show ordered a lime green outfit for myself, which I eventually donated to the Arizona Costume Institute in Phoenix.) After a few more sequences of exciting color, eight models appeared together wearing very sophisticated black dresses, all slim and to the knee, accessorized only with dramatic black hats. Then came an innocent looking group of white dresses detailed with tucks and white lace. All the collection was perfectly accessorized. Valentino was a master. He ended the show with spectacular evening gowns, some floaty beaded chiffons, others slim colorful silks.

While the show progressed, Franca leaned over and whispered to me, "Ollie, the elegant women in Rome have already discovered Valentino and are wearing his clothes to all the important social events and private clubs. You are the first American buyer to see Valentino's collection."

Franca smiled as she spoke, "He is really talented and will be famous someday. I'm happy to see you recognize and appreciate his style."

By the time the show had ended, I was ready to place my order. Valentino insisted we have lunch first, and as we ate he confessed he had never been to the United States. A year later, I was greeting him at my front door in New York. He had learned enough English that we could communicate, and to make things easier I made reservations at a very good Italian restaurant. That was the beginning of our friendship and business relationship. It didn't take long for the Valentino name to become famous, worldwide. To this day I reminisce about that incredible first collection presented to us when, for just a few moments, I felt like a queen on her throne.

I returned to New York, exhausted, and coping with the time change, to find a message for me regarding a penthouse apartment I was interested in renting. Already I had outgrown my one room, and was anxious to move into larger quarters. Since it was a rent-controlled building, it was affordable. I called Eloise Curtis, one of my designer friends, who lived there and had promised to let me have the place when she was ready to move.

"We've decided to move, Ollie, and you can have the penthouse if you still want it," she said, "but please come up today because the landlord will rent it immediately if he finds out we're leaving."

We made a date to meet at her place in an hour. When I arrived, Eloise was already there. Since the rental office was on premise, she took me to the landlord to fill out the necessary papers. He was satisfied with my credentials and Eloise's recommendation, so I was now officially the new tenant. Eloise was moving in a month, so I notified my landlord I would be leaving at the end of my lease, which was six weeks away. I was so happy. The penthouse was on East 55th Street in a tall building, so the panoramic view on three sides of the huge terrace was unobstructed. The ceilings were about sixteen feet high with tall windows overlooking the terrace. It was very light and airy. There was a fireplace on one wall of the spacious living room and French doors leading outside. The floors throughout were parquet. The bedroom was quite large with tall windows overlooking the terrace. The kitchen was small but adequate.

Moving from the studio apartment to my enormous penthouse was easy because both locations were in the same part of town. What little furniture I owned was placed in the living room like stray orphans swallowed up by space. I needed everything. The bedroom was totally empty and the entry foyer and living room looked barren. The first purchase I made, however, was not for those rooms. It was for the patio. I couldn't wait to lie out there on my Woodard wrought iron furniture luxuriating in the outdoors. Such a rarity in New York City—your own piece of sunshine just outside the door.

That summer, I was vacationing in East Hampton and decided to drive to Shelter Island to look around. The Island is at the tip of Long Island and can be reached only by ferry from both the North and South shores. I liked it there, because it was quiet and away from the Hamptons where there was always a party. I noticed a "For Sale" sign on a quaint little house that really appealed to me. Even though I wasn't looking, I called the phone number on the sign and within a half hour the owner of the house arrived. She was anxious to sell because she was moving to Minnesota. The price she quoted was so low that I didn't even counter and bought it based on a thorough inspection. I had decided to look for a weekend-summer house for some time and this one just appeared. Now I was a home-owner for the first time. I would need to completely furnish it, and also find a car to get around the island.

I found the car in Palm Beach a few months later when I was scheduled to visit the Saks Fifth Avenue Florida stores. While in Palm Beach, I once again bumped into my friend, Freddie Pomerantz. He drove up to the hotel just as I arrived, driving a little beach buggy.

"Hey, Freddie, that's just what I need on Shelter Island," I remarked. "I bought a house there and need some kind of transportation. Where can I buy one?"

"Buy one!" he said. "You can have this one. I'll even ship it to New York for you. You'd be doing me a favor taking it off my hands."

Ollie in her Fiat, "Jolly"

Several weeks later, when the buggy arrived in New York, a friend of mine and I drove it to Shelter Island. For the next few years that little beach buggy, a Fiat Jolly with a fringed canvas top and open sides, became the hit of the island. No one had ever seen another one like it.

This was now the late fifties. I was immersed in my work six days a week, bringing reports home each evening and on weekends to analyze. There were never enough hours in the day. I was dating a little, but nothing serious, until I was introduced to John Wright. We met through Dick Edwards, a mutual friend, at the Artist and Writer's Club, a restaurant-bar they liked.

"Meet you at the bar at one o'clock and we'll have lunch," Dick said.

My first impression of John was not a lasting one. He seemed a little Eastern prep school cocky that day, and I was turned off by some of his flip remarks. He was handsome, about six feet tall, blonde hair, and laughed throughout lunch. He had beautiful teeth. He was wearing a tweed jacket, grey flannel pants, and a red striped tie. He sat in a sideways, slumped position, sort of looking over his shoulder at me.

"Ollie, when can we see each other without Edwards around?" John asked about an hour later.

"Give me a call, and we can talk about it," I replied handing him one of my business cards. "I need to dash off to an appointment now. It was nice meeting you. Goodbye."

He called later that day and we made a date for the following evening.

Little did I know, until after a few dates, how much John traveled. He would be in town for a week and gone for three. On the weekends he was home, we would fly to Shelter Island. He owned his own plane, and often the weather would be zero-zero, with us flying in the muck searching for God-sent holes in the clouds in order to land. I was totally scared to death each time it happened. He just laughed. "Luck of the Irish," he would proclaim jubilantly. Each time it happened I swore I would never go up in that plane again. We dated for about a year, then a short break, on again, off again, on again. I noticed what a heavy drinker he was and that he spent much of his time while home in his favorite bars. Subconsciously, he reminded me of my father, who never stopped drinking until the day he died. No one could convince him to stop. In time, we all gave up trying. I should have known better, but John was a charmer, sober or drunk. When he proposed after a particularly sweet period, I accepted. Don't ask me why, but I believed him when he promised the impossible: to reform. Ha, Ha, Ha, Ha! I wanted to believe him. I didn't know alcoholism was an addiction, a sickness, a disease. Only John could change himself. It was the early sixties, and terms like "alcoholic," "the program," "twelve steps," "powerlessness," "power greater than ourselves," were not used as openly as they are today. I was foolish enough to think I could change him and get him to stop drinking all by myself. All I had to do was marry him and love him. Then, if I played God, I might perform miracles. Naturally, nothing worked.

We dated for about a year. He traveled half that time, and when he was home I would prepare gourmet dinners by candlelight and dress up in some lovely at-home outfit. He never showed up when expected. An hour or two later, I would call Dick Edwards' bar and there he would be.

"I'm coming. I'm coming home, sweetheart. See you in a half hour," He was drunk. When he arrived home, flushed and smiling his feeling-guilty-grin, he would give me a hug and a kiss and, "I'm sorry, Honey," worthy of an Academy Award.

We were married in a private ceremony out on Long Island. Cathy Apothaker, (my assistant, now married) was matron-of-honor and Dick Edwards was

John Wright, Cindy's dad

John's best man. We had a long-weekend honeymoon, and then John left on another trip. (He worked for King Features Syndicate selling syndicated columns and features to newspapers in his Mid-West territory.) He moved in with me shortly before we were married. It didn't take long for me to discover drinking-John continued to be drinking-John, and traveling-John continued to be traveling-John. He still spent most of his time at Dick Edwards' bar, but he would return home, face flushed and grinning like a clown, to proclaim his undying love. He reminded me of my father, so many years before, staggering home from the bar, face flushed, grinning like a clown, pleading with me to remove his smelly shoes and socks.

A few months later, while he was traveling, I realized I was pregnant. Totally unexpected! I didn't tell many people, but it wasn't too long before I began to show. No hiding it now; I was in full bloom. Trudging through the market with my new silhouette slowed me down, but I worked right up to the day Cindy was born. She surprised us all that morning, January 14, 1961 at 9:19 a.m.; she weighed only four pounds, eleven ounces and was immediately whisked off to be placed in an incubator in intensive care, unbeknownst to me. I thought they had lost her.

I was in a state of panic when I didn't see her in the room and screamed hysterically at the nurses, "Where is my baby? What have you done to her? Why have you taken her from my room?" I was sitting upright in bed, anxious to hold her. "I want to see her! Has she died and you don't want to tell me?"

Two nurses rushed to my room to calm me down and reassure me my baby was fine. "Show her to me!" I demanded, "I don't believe you!"

The nurses finally quieted me down enough to tell me all babies under five pounds are put in an incubator. Fortunately, they examine these babies thoroughly, and in so doing discovered Cindy was born with several heart defects called tetralogy of fallot. She had a hole in her heart, very narrow veins, and would require open heart surgery when she reached six years of age. They could not perform such intensive surgery on an infant.

When I finally saw Cindy for the first time, I was struck by how tiny she was. She could easily fit in the palm of my hand. She looked normal except for slightly blue fingertips and toes. She looked up at me from the incubator, her little arms flailing, and her eyes focused on mine. I wondered what she saw, and convinced myself she instinctively knew I was her mother. Tears welled up in my eyes. How I ached to pick her up and hold her, but I was told that would take a few more days. I was released from the hospital later that day and began my daily trips from home to see Cindy in the hospital. When the nurse finally put her in my arms for the first time, it was, and always will be, the most precious moment of my life. She was completely bald except for peach fuzz, with the softest pink cheeks, and sparkling eyes that lit up her entire face when she smiled.

Two weeks later, John and I brought Cindy home to the penthouse apartment, where her crib was set up in our bedroom. She looked like a tiny China doll in that huge crib. Knowing she would require twenty-four hour care, we luckily found Gerda Niebuhr for the job. She was highly recommended by a mutual friend who knew her from a previous position. It wasn't long before we observed her instinctive tenderness towards Cindy and her German cleanliness. Gerda was in her late twenties, about five feet, five inches tall, with light brown hair. It was important that Cindy not catch any respiratory diseases her first year, so we were very careful. Her nurse worked all

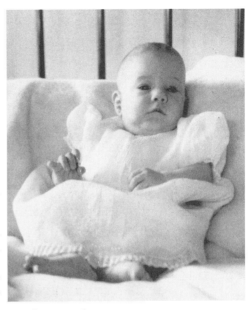

Cindy as an infant

day and I took over evenings and weekends. Cindy blossomed her first year, and before we knew it, she was crawling all over the apartment. We knew we needed a bigger place, at least something with two bedrooms, so I started looking in the newspaper. I looked for weeks.

At last, there it was! A brownstone house on East Eighty-Fourth Street, described as a tear-down, was surprisingly inexpensive and available immediately. I called the owner and made arrangements to meet at the building the following morning. The location between First and Second Avenue turned out to be a lovely residential neighborhood, and the building definitely needed to be torn down and renovated. I asked for the lowest price he would accept, and after a little negotiating arrived at a sum I could work with. I was ecstatic to "own" my own place in Manhattan at 350 East 84th Street. To raise money, I decided to sell my house on Shelter Island or place a first and second mortgage on the property. I would also need a hefty sum to pay for the renovation. The building was four stories high, twenty feet wide, and forty feet deep, but the property itself was one hundred feet deep. I planned to make two duplexes, rent the upper one and live in the lower one. (Rent-producing property provided a good tax advantage for me.)

Now my search for a good architect and contractor began. I asked all my friends on Seventh Avenue, as well as personal friends, and eventually found two young architects who were partners in their own firm. God has always worked in my life, and at this precise time, I was told about three brownstone houses, adjacent to one another, being demolished on East 64th Street. They were owned by Myron Taylor, who lived in the middle building and left the other two vacant for visitors. When he died, he donated the buildings to the Catholic Church. The Church sold the properties and the new owner decided to demolish them. A friend of mine saw an ad in the *New York Times* that read, "Merchandise Available. Architectural pieces and ornaments. You dismantle and remove and it's yours." The address was the Myron Taylor home. My friend and I rushed up to the house and were stupefied by our good fortune. Myron Taylor had a passion for antique European, architectural, unique pieces, and as we ran from room to room, we gasped with pleasure. It was better than any Roman feast! The workmen were beginning to demolish, so we got serious and down to business. I ended up buying one-third of a Fourteenth-Century beamed and carved ceiling, with painted coffers in between the beams, approximately thirty feet long. I also bought thirty feet of the antique Italian marble ballroom floor. The ceiling eventually became the living room ceiling in my brownstone. The marble floor was used in the family room, and I had it installed on the outdoor patio when we extended the building. It was a deep greeny-black marble with an aged luster. I purchased the main door and the side door and used them as entrances to both duplexes. They were thick, heavy doors with a little window to see "Who's there?" They had a built-in, ancient, inner-sanctum squeeeeeak. There were a trio of incredibly detailed, wrought-iron window guards that I had made to fit one entire wall on the ground floor leading to the patio and garden. Every curly-cue of the filigreed detailing ended with a miniature horse's head. They were very old and completely crafted by gifted hands. These guards protected the mottled, antique leaded-glass windows I also purchased. Upstairs in the master bedroom, I had very tall ceilings to accommodate the ceiling-to–floor, colorful leaded glass windows that opened like doors, with set leaded glass windows above. They were spectacular, especially when the early morning sunshine poured in, spraying irregular splashes of color on the king-size bed, the floor, and the walls. I purchased every leaded glass window at the site, and also some interior doors. (These I was able to take with me when I eventually moved to Arizona and use them in our home there.) Fortunately, I had the basement of my brownstone house to store all these purchases until needed for installation. My friend and I somehow managed to hire people to remove the items and truck them to our homes, all intact and miraculously each in one piece.

Now, we needed a contractor. Through friends we met and hired an Italian contractor, Angelo Ferlito, who bid on the job along with two others. The construction began and moved smoothly for several months, until workmen stopped showing up and Angelo disappeared. It was impossible to reach him by phone or at his home on Long Island. We lost about a week of work. When he returned, he asked for a sizeable payment which was not yet due. I told him he would be paid when the work was done.

"No money, no work," he said, "I send my men to another job, unless you pay me now."

I was frantic and paid him half of what he demanded. Things went smoothly for awhile and then the same thing happened. No Angelo. No workmen. He began complaining that he had underbid the job and was losing money. He walked off the job and took his men with him. We found someone to complete the building, but I was in court with Angelo not too long after he left and through arbitration settled the matter. He had turned into a raging bull, and I was glad to be rid of him!

Finally the building was finished, and it looked beautiful. We used old brick for the front and back and installed a wrought iron stairway outside for access to the upper duplex. The back of the building overlooked a twenty-by-forty private garden that had three mature trees, a lawn, and a marble patio where I often read the Sunday *Times* and had breakfast while Cindy played with her toys. The first floor had Cindy's bedroom, bathroom, the kitchen, and a large family room leading out to the patio. By extending the building twenty feet, we were able to have this room and a roof-top patio for the upper duplex, which I rented to a young couple when the building was completed. The second floor had a thirty-foot living room, with antique beamed ceiling beautifully installed, a large master bedroom, and a bathroom.

For awhile we were happy there, but I never felt like a family. John was constantly traveling, and he much preferred flying to Shelter Island than staying in the city when he was home. Since I worked all week, I flew out on the weekends with Cindy and Gerda. One weekend I decided to fly out alone on a commuter flight and surprise John. We would have the entire weekend to ourselves, something we hadn't enjoyed in a long time. I arranged to be dropped off at the house by a friend and when I walked in John wasn't there. "Maybe he's in the guest house," I thought. As I walked through the breezeway, I could hear noises inside, and laughter. "I wonder who that could be at this time of day." I opened the door, and to my horror, there he was totally naked with a young trollop from the village, also totally naked, going at it full force.

He instantly sat upright in bed, struggled to cover himself with a sheet, and with a very flushed face and slurring words, looked at me in disbelief. "What are you doing here? My God, what are you doing here? You're not supposed to be here." He looked and sounded like an old fool.

It was obvious they were both drunk and unprepared for my surprise arrival. I was totally shocked. For a moment I wanted to throw something at them, a chair or a lamp. Instead, I screamed at her to get out, get out, GET OUT. She jumped out of bed naked and ran for the bathroom door. That was the last I saw of her.

It never occurred to me that John would ever be unfaithful to me. Me, dedicated wife, mother, career woman. Me, little Miss Perfect, true blue, upstanding citizen. Me, stay-at-home, waiting by the telephone, believing in him . Maybe that was the problem. "I'll never, ever trust you again, John. Never," I screamed as loud as I could. "I'll leave in the morning. You can start planning on packing and moving out as soon as you get back to New York. It's ended."

On the flight back, I thought about John and me. We really weren't happy together. Ours was hardly a marriage made in heaven. The face-to-face encounter with this girl made me wonder how many women there were on John's various business trips. He was obviously quite the ladies' man. He spent very little time with Cindy and me, preferring to be with his drinking buddies in New York and Shelter Island. It wasn't long before John and I grew apart. It took the shock of finding him in bed with another woman to face that reality. His drinking was really beginning to bother me, making a stranger out of a husband. He preferred Dick Edwards' bar and his Remy Martin, VSOP, extra dry, martinis to staying at home with us. When I asked him for a divorce, he refused, claiming he loved me and Cindy. I could see no future in the relationship and asked Dick Edwards, John's best friend, to please help move him out. He finally left; during the next few months we completed a property settlement and I flew off to Mexico for the formal divorce. (New York State didn't recognize incompatibility as reason enough for a divorce, and at that time many people flew down for legal "Mexican Divorces.") This all happened in 1964. We had been married a little over four years.

I was working full-time during the renovation of the building, but I went to the site every morning at seven, during my lunch, and every evening before going home. Much of the weekend was spent with the architects, and we somehow managed to complete the project in eight months. We couldn't move in until the building department approved the entire job and gave us the coveted "Certificate of Occupancy." I was told that I should hand over a hefty sum of money in an envelope to the inspector.

When he arrived, several weeks later, I very awkwardly blurted out, "I was told to give this to you or I won't get my certificate, and I need to move in with my little baby daughter who has a heart problem, and my lease is up in three days. So here!"

With that, I started to cry so hard, I couldn't control the sobs. I had never done anything like that before. Luckily for me, the inspector was very kind.

He took my hand and returned the envelope saying, "This isn't necessary. Your building is approved and I will expedite the paper work so you and your daughter can move in two days."

I have never forgotten that.

SIX

From John to Gerry

Men in My Life

Two days later we received our Certificate of Occupancy and were ready to go. The movers arrived at the penthouse at eight o'clock in the morning, and after the truck was loaded I took a taxi and met them at the Brownstone. After all the furniture and boxes were unloaded, I was amazed at how much room we had. It was spacious and cozy at the same time. I returned to pick up Cindy and Gerda and was anxious to see their reactions to our new home. Of course, Cindy ran from room to room, and then headed for the stairs. I took her by the hand and the two of us walked upstairs together.

"Ooooo, Mommy, look at the pretty windows," Cindy cooed. "Do we live here now?"

"Do you like it, sweetheart?" I replied.

"Oh, yes," she answered, "Show me my bedroom."

As we descended, Cindy couldn't contain her enthusiasm.

"Gerda, Gerda, where are you? Come see my bedroom. Mommy knows where it is."

Gerda was at the foot of the stairs waiting for us, and she swooped Cindy up in her arms and led her to the bedroom she would share with her. Everybody was happy, particularly me, because all the work and time dedicated to the construction was over. I don't know what I would have done without Gerda. She helped with the unpacking, stayed longer hours, and watched Cindy as she ran up and down the hallway. She cooked, cleaned, and did the laundry without being asked. She had such a pleasant disposition, and nothing was too much for her.

Months later, I invited one of my talented designer friends for dinner at the brownstone.

He couldn't believe what had been accomplished and in his enthusiasm blurted out, "Ollie, this would be a fabulous setting for a fashion show, and I'd love to present my new collection right here in your living room. We can move what little furniture you have in there and set up little gold, folding chairs. The room can easily hold a hundred people. What do you think?"

I loved the idea, so we sat down that same evening and planned our opening party. All week we worked on the guest list and the invitation. We decided to play up the location by describing the "Fourteenth Century beamed-and-coffered-ceiling living room as the setting for the Fashion Show," and, "Enjoying antique ironwork, massive European entry doors, and soaring leaded-glass windows, as you browse through both floors of this renovated brownstone." We invited the press, about a hundred clients, and a few close friends. Almost everyone we invited accepted, including the fashion editors of *Vogue, Bazaar, Town and Country, Glamour, Mademoiselle, Women's Wear Daily*, and the *New York Times*. They all loved it and suggested we make it an annual event.

My housewarming party, however, held during Christmas season a few months later, was the biggest success. We decorated every room in the house, up the stairway banister, and used the big tree outside the family room as the "Christmas tree." It was totally covered with blinking bee lights. During the day it started to snow, and the effect of snowflakes falling softly and bee lights flickering on and off, seen through the leaded-glass windows in the family room and master bedroom, was breathtaking.

The Christmas table was set up in the living room, with a suckling pig as the centerpiece surrounded by huge candles and laden with turkey, ham, cranberry sauce, vegetables, salads, fresh breads and rolls. A second table was filled with unusual holiday desserts including cakes, pastries, fruit, and nuts. Its centerpiece was a magnificent raspberry milles feuilles, a puff pastry tart big enough to serve the whole party. The bar was set up in the family room, but waiters floated around serving drinks all evening. Light drinkers loved the punch, concocted with rosé wine, ginger ale, and something else fizzy. I invited about forty of my favorite people, and since many had not seen the house before, I found myself giving personal tours and regaling them with stories about the construction.

That housewarming party was the second big event I held in the house, though there were many candlelit dinners for four or six during the five years we lived there. Cindy was always allowed to meet guests during the early evening, because she was polite and friendly. We would dress her up in her little dresses, tights, and maryjanes and she would charm everyone. Gerda was always close by.

During those years in the Brownstone, Cindy and I used to go to the park near Gracie Square located in the Eighties near the East River. She loved being pushed in her stroller and stopping to feed the birds. We would bring a baggie full of bird food, and she would clutch it tightly until bird-time came. My friends, Lewis Kozer and John Brunelle, spent occasional Sundays at the house with us. They adored Cindy. One Easter we all went to brunch at Sign of the Dove dressed in our new Easter outfits. Cindy wore a bright yellow coat with matching yellow bonnet, little white gloves, white tights, and black patent-leather shoes. She had all eyes on her when she walked in. During brunch she decided she wanted to walk around the restaurant.

"Mommy, may I see the restaurant and look at the people?" she asked politely.

"Only if you don't disturb anyone," I replied.

She turned out to be the hit of the Easter Brunch. Table after table called her over and talked to her. Cindy wasn't bashful, and she carried on conversations with total strangers. We watched her as she flitted like a little bird, smiling with her familiar light-up-your-face smile. We decided attention had transformed her into a miniature hostess. When she finally returned to our table, she was elated and very talkative.

"That lady over there said she liked my dress, Mommy. And that man over there said he wished he had a little granddaughter like me. Isn't that nice? Guess what? She gave me this little chocolate bunny!"

When we were finished with brunch and were walking out, Cindy-the-star-of-the-day blew kisses to these new friends who applauded her as she left.

It was a memorable day for her, and for weeks we called her our little movie star. Gerda loved the story when we told her about it the following day.

"Cindy may look shy but she is very open and friendly and happy all day long," Gerda told me.

"I know, and much of that is due to the love and kindness you always give her." I replied. "We are very lucky to have found you, Gerda." And I gave her a great big hug. With my all-consuming career demanding so much time, it was a huge relief to have a reliable person taking care of Cindy. It was particularly hectic during Market Week.

In those days, the Fall Market opened in early May. That meant I would attend a series of formal fashion shows in the vendor showrooms or in theatres that held more people. As the buyer for Saks Fifth Avenue, I was always given front row center seats. Out of courtesy I made a point of being prompt or a bit early. There was usually a bit of a fuss, as I would slither down on my seat, and the huggy-kissy-cheeks moment would pass.

"Hi, Jane," "How are you, Bill?" "What's new in Dallas?"

I would answer the hellos in my vicinity. I really liked most of the buyers I met over the years. They came from all over the world representing big stores or their own businesses. We were all there for the same reason: to buy the right clothes for the season and to select styles for advertising purposes. There was always a sense of anticipation and excitement before every show. The houselights would go off, the music would blare, and the show would begin. I'd make an occasional notation, but my "buy" didn't happen until the "writing appointment," already scheduled for the following day. At that time, the salesman who took care of our account would be ready for us with all the collection hanging on racks. I'd go through the clothes, quickly selecting the styles I liked, and put them on a separate rack. Models were on hand in case I wanted to see something on the body again. I preferred to try them on myself to get the feeling of the cut of a jacket or a top. This helped, because I could catch something I might not notice otherwise, like a sleeve that was too wide or a cut that looked matronly on a normal size 8 body. I had a reputation for being the fastest buyer to buy a line. I just didn't waste any time.

After I edited my selection, wrote styles, descriptions, and prices on worksheets, I was ready to leave for my next appointment. This generally took about one hour. I would collect all my worksheets each day and work on them in the evening. "Working on them" meant retailing each style and breaking down the quantities. Since I was buying for twenty stores, each store had a separate budget. I would buy by store, beginning with the smallest and working up to the biggest. This was time consuming, but I ensured that each store received a reasonable assortment instead of a haphazard selection. When all the worksheets were completed and the cost was computed, I would begin cutting some styles if we were overbought. I always left enough money in my budget for reorders. It was this tedious, careful buying that was the secret of our success, because it reduced markdowns and ultimately gave the department its high profitability.

It was after one of these fashion shows that a store owner from Phoenix, Arizona, came up to me and introduced himself. I was taken by surprise because we had seen each other in the market over the years but had never spoken. He approached with a big smile.

"Hi, Ollie, I'm Gerry McNamara," he said, oozing with charm. "I have an appointment with Adam Gimbel (the president of Saks Fifth Avenue) this afternoon and thought I'd stop by your office when I'm finished. Will you be back about four-thirty?"

I thought to myself, "My, he's attractive. I wonder what he has in mind." I replied, "I should be back by then. It's so difficult to find a cab after four o'clock in the market, I try to return to the store by that time."

Later that afternoon when I returned, Gerry was waiting for me in my department. He wore a perfectly tailored, double-breasted, navy and white striped suit with a hot pink shirt which must have been custom-made because it had no extra fabric and fit tightly on his body. I liked the widespread collar, rather than ordinary button-down type so many men wore. His tie, a bright multi diagnol stripe, was perfect. As a last touch, he carelessly tucked a foulard pocket scarf into his breast pocket. What taste! I later found out he used Oleg Cassini's tailor in Italy and had his shirts made at Turnbull and Asser in London.

We sat in my office and Gerry asked, "Did you know Adam Gimbel was planning to build a Saks Fifth Avenue store in Phoenix? He offered me the management position."

"But don't you already own your own store there?" I asked with some curiosity.

"Yes, I do, but Mr. Gimbel offered to buy my store and all the inventory. The whole deal is almost too good to turn down."

He looked at me as though I would, somehow, know the right answer.

"You would be a nice addition to Saks," I said. "But that's a big decision only you can make."

"You're right, of course, but you're one of the buyers in the market whose opinion I respect, and beside that, I thought we could get to know one another better." He threw that in quickly, and then added, "You don't happen to be free for dinner tonight, do you? I'm only in town for a few days and would love to take you to my favorite little Italian restaurant."

I slowly checked my date calendar, knowing full well I was free, and answered, "That sounds like fun. Shall we say around eight at my place?"

That evening I found I was really excited about my new date. I decided to wear the New York uniform little-black-dress with my double strand of pearls and big, round pearl earrings. Since it was a little chilly, I decided to wear my new, sensational red coat over it. My hair was short at that time, brunette with blonde streaks. Just as I finished dressing, the doorbell rang, promptly at eight o'clock. When I opened the door, there was Gerry with his arms full of flowers, chocolates, and a bottle of champagne.

"Wow! You really know how to treat a girl!" I laughed.

"Ollie, I couldn't wait to see you tonight. You really look beautiful."

He gave me a little kiss on the cheek, and we walked down the hallway to the family room. He asked about the entrance door. Where did I find such a spectacular piece?

"My God," he exclaimed when he spotted the wall of antique iron gates, "These are incredible! Look at the horse's heads." He obviously loved antiques. "Do you mind showing me the second floor?"

When he saw the beamed ceiling in the living room, and the leaded-glass windows in the bedroom, he was really impressed. We went back downstairs and I suggested we have a glass of wine before leaving.

"I can't get over your beautiful home," he remarked. "Not too many people have access to these architectural antique pieces. Where did you find them?"

"It was my lucky day," I replied. "A friend of mine saw the ad in the *New York Times* and asked if I would like to see what was available. We went up to the location immediately and were thrilled to find what we did. It's a long story I can tell you at dinner."

Gerry was curious. "You have wonderful taste and your home reflects that. I'd like to see everything you found." He walked slowly over, put his arms around me, looked deeply into my eyes and kissed me several times.

"We'll never leave at this rate," I said.

"I don't mind," Gerry whispered in my ear. "You give me goose bumps just being near you."

He was mesmerizing. Any minute I expected him to unzip my dress. Instead, we finished our drinks and left for the Italian restaurant he'd mentioned earlier. I had never been there, even though it was quite close to home. As we entered we were greeted with open arms and infectious, Italian enthusiasm. "Gerry, my friend, how good to see you again. And who is this beautiful lady you have brought to us?"

"Giorgio, this is Ollie, and tonight we are enjoying our first date. Ollie, meet Giorgio, the owner of this charming restaurant. By the way, do you have any more of that delicious Chianti I had the other night?"

"Sure, sure, I bring it right away," he replied. "Let me put you at your favorite table."

Romantic Italian music played softly in the background and candles flickered on the tables. The room was warm and cozy. As I looked around, I saw that every table was taken. I turned and looked at Gerry. "I love being here with you," he said quietly. "Here's to you and to us." As we sipped the velvety red wine I knew this evening was just the beginning.

"Is there anything special you like to eat here?" I asked

"I always order their spaghetti Bolognese. It's the best I've ever eaten," said Gerry.

"That's okay with me. I'd like to start with an arugula and watercress salad." I was getting hungry, and the wine was beginning to make me slightly light-headed. By now we were holding hands, and Gerry's rugged face was slightly flushed. He ordered the same salad. I thought to myself, as I gazed at him, how handsome he was. I liked his ready smile and the way his soft grey eyes crinkled when he laughed. He was very intense when he talked and totally charming. He admitted he was married, in the process of separating, and that he had two daughters. He and his wife owned a small retail store in Phoenix, Arizona, called Gerry McNamara.

"I could sit here looking at you all evening," he said. Once again he leaned over and kissed me. Our heads were very close, so I slowly sat upright.

"What is happening with your marriage, Gerry? Are you serious about a breakup?"

"We've been having personal problems for the last year," he replied, "so when Adam Gimbel proposed my joining Saks and selling our store to him, it was as though fate stepped in. Our store was run by both of us, so this would be a clean break." He seemed anxious to tell me all this and, by the time we left the restaurant, I felt I'd known him for years instead of just hours.

We walked home hand-in-hand and since it was quite late we said good night at the door and made plans for the following evening.

"About eight?" he asked, putting his arms around me and kissing me several times.

"That's fine," I whispered. "See you tomorrow."

About twenty minutes later the phone rang. It was Gerry.

"I just had to talk to you again, to tell you how much I enjoyed the evening. I'm staying here at Oleg's, (Oleg Cassini, the designer) an old friend of mine. Why don't you meet me here for a drink tomorrow and we'll go to dinner afterwards. Maybe we can end the evening dancing at Le Club."

"That sounds like a fun evening," I said sleepily. "Let me jot down the address and phone number, and I'll meet you there around eight."

The following morning I was busy at work when Gerry called.

"Let's have lunch together. I know a nice little place within walking distance of the store. I'll meet you there around twelve. Okay?"

"Okay," I replied, "but I have to be back at the store by one-fifteen for an appointment."

The morning flew by, and the next thing I knew I was sitting, holding hands with Gerry in a little French restaurant.

He ordered lunch immediately and then, gazing deeply into my eyes, said, "Since last night, all I've been able to think about is you. I would love to paint you, and try to capture your beautiful face, and delicate skin tones. Let's spend the weekend together. I'll pick up a canvas, some paints and brushes, and I'll paint you standing against your lovely leaded-glass windows with just the right light touching you."

"I didn't know you painted," I remarked. "Where did you study?"

"I went to the Art Student's League for a few years, and knew from the beginning art was my true love. I just can't make a living painting."

At that moment lunch arrived, and we continued our conversation about his painting, the weekend, and changing his reservations back to Phoenix from Friday to Tuesday. When we finished lunch, we walked back to the store holding hands, and kissed goodbye-see-you-tonight.

That evening, as I rang the doorbell at Oleg's place, I expected Gerry to answer. Much to my surprise, a gorgeous girl answered and invited me in.

"I'm here to meet Gerry McNamara," I said, and noticed three other beautiful girls draped on the couch in the living room.

They all introduced themselves as friends of Oleg's. They were models from Europe, and were house guests of Oleg's. At that moment, Gerry walked in, gave me a hug and a kiss, and introduced me to the group. A few minutes later, Oleg came in, having just taken a shower, and tucking in his custom-made shirt, said hello. With his Russian polish and chiseled good looks, he leaned over and kissed my hand. I couldn't stop thinking whether he had just "done it" with the Latvian girl or the brunette from Iceland. Or two at a time. I even wondered where Gerry fit into this picture. It felt very strange. We all had a glass of wine together, and then Gerry and I were off.

"We'll meet you at Le Club later," Gerry said in parting, "around eleven."

We walked to a restaurant in midtown and after dinner took a cab to Le Club. The place was packed, and you were required to check in at the door for admittance. Finally inside, we found a booth, ordered some wine, and tried to talk above the loud disco music. It wasn't easy. I've never seen so many beautiful people speaking so many different languages in one place. It was the hot spot of the moment, and if you didn't belong, you weren't "in." That is what it was like in New York in the late fifties and early sixties: Chubby Checker and the Twist, The Cotton Club in Harlem, Jazz, and the Blues. I remember seeing Lena Horne perform at the Waldorf and how unforgettable she was, and also seeing Harry Belafonte, young and very handsome. Dancing in the Cub Room at the Stork Club meant you were somebody or you knew somebody. They just didn't let anybody in. Same at El Morocco. Nightclubs, supper clubs, piano bars, cocktail lounges all added to the nightlife of the time. Le Club was an instant hit when it opened, and Gerry joined as an out-of-town member.

As we were talking the music softened. "Let's dance," said Gerry. "I want to hold you in my arms." As we slowly moved around the floor, he whispered, "How does spending the weekend together sound to you?" I'd love to," I replied. By now the music, the wine, the ambience, and the man had all begun to affect me.

We spent every minute of that weekend together. Gerry picked up the painting materials, and began a nude study of me the following day with early morning light streaming through the leaded-glass windows. He liked to paint with classical music playing, so we selected some favorite records and soon Gerry was lost in his own world. In the afternoon we ate a picnic lunch in the garden and then sank into love land on my big king-size bed. We spent quite a bit of time there over the weekend. In between we sipped wine, ate pasta, took walks, and finished the painting. By Sunday night we were planning when we would see each other again.

"Can you meet me in Palm Springs the end of this month? I'm playing in a polo tournament there and would love to have you fly out for a long weekend. Do you think you can make it?"

I wasn't sure. "That sounds wonderful, but I'll have to check my work schedule. Call me tomorrow night and I'll let you know."

We did see each other that weekend, and others as well. We flew to Jackson Hole, Wyoming, to stay with Paul von Gontard and used his log-cabin-like guest house for several days. Paul was a dashing friend of Gerry's who lived in Phoenix, Arizona, when he wasn't in Jackson Hole. They both went riding daily, and since I was afraid of those big

Gerry McNamara, James' dad

animals, I would stay behind and read. The romance flourished with each contact. In between, we wrote letters or telephoned on a daily basis. Gerry asked his wife for a divorce. Though I felt very much like the "other woman," I was told over and over again it was going to happen with or without me in the picture. I wasn't so sure but, by now, we were very much in love, and being together was most important.

I thought I had met the man of my dreams, and when he proposed, I accepted. That opened up a whole new set of problems. He lived in Phoenix and I lived in New York. Who moves where? I really loved my job and had a bright future with Saks Fifth Avenue. Could I bear to give up the thrill of future accomplishments, my financial independence, and the prestige of my position? I would have to sell my brownstone that I loved so dearly. Would I ever regret doing that? Most importantly, how would this all affect Cindy? Gerry had another set of problems. If he moved to New York, his future career was up in the air. His financial dilemma now included child support and alimony. His two young daughters would not see their father for long periods of time. Marrying Gerry meant change, big change, and Gerry and I talked about this over and over again. When his divorce was final, he found an apartment in Phoenix to live in temporarily until we could sort things out. He would do whatever I decided, so it was up to me. I gave the most thought to Cindy. She was three years old now and soon would be in school. Her open heart surgery would happen when she turned six. I wondered about heart specialists in Phoenix. Would Cindy thrive more in the "small town" atmosphere of Phoenix, with big, grassy backyards, horses, cats, and dogs, public schools she could eventually bicycle to, a pool to learn how to swim in, and best of all, mommy staying at home full time?

"Cindy," I asked her, "how would you like to move to Arizona with me? Gerry has asked me to marry him, and I wondered how you would like him to be your new daddy."

"I'd like him to be my new daddy." Cindy replied, "He said he would teach me how to ride a horse, so let's go to Arizona."

Cindy in Phoenix, Gerry taught her to ride when she was this little

Every moment I spent with Cindy, I realized how much I enjoyed being with her and how much I loved her. Whenever I visited the branch stores and was gone a week or longer, I missed her desperately.

Each trip, as I was leaving, Cindy would run down the hallway with arms outstretched sobbing, "Mommy, Mommy, don't go, don't go!" It broke my heart every time.

I began to think about the marriage, the move, the future, and came to the conclusion that spending every day with my daughter was far more important than my career or the brownstone. Cindy helped make my decision. I didn't say anything to Gerry for a few days. I wanted to make sure about this move. The first person I called was my best friend, Cathy Apothaker, who lived in Philadelphia.

She and I weighed the pros and cons, and her final remark, "Ollie, this is a decision only you can make. It's a big one," left me just where I had started.

Everything seemed to be happening so fast. I began to feel emotionally trapped, like I did with husband number one, Judah

Holstein. I took pride in my decisiveness, sensibleness, and intelligence, but these qualities had nothing to do with my feelings. Gerry was all about feelings. How could I run away from the life I had built over the past fifteen years, move two thousand miles away, and start a new life. Of course I could; I was in love. What stronger pull had control over me?

Even the church had abandoned me. When I couldn't obtain an annulment from Judah, I was told by the priests I could never remarry in the Catholic Church. I could not receive the sacraments and, in reality, I was "excommunicated" from the church. For

Cindy as a little girl in the back yard of the brownstone house I purchased and renovated

months afterwards, I felt like a doomed sinner. I gave up going to daily Mass and receiving communion. It was a dark period for me, and when I met Gerry, I felt alright again. I was not defective. He saw all my good qualities and made me feel whole. It wasn't until two other people I spoke to said pretty much the same. They couldn't believe I'd give up life in New York to move to Phoenix, Arizona! I prayed over it, and finally made my decision. I would marry Gerry. He was elated when I told him.

"Ollie, you've made me very happy," he told me by phone from Arizona, "and I'll dedicate my life to you and Cindy. I love you both very much. I've been looking for a house here and think I've found just the right place. Now that you've decided to marry me and move to Phoenix, I'll make an offer." Which he did, and within a week the details were completed and he owned the house. Now everything was up to me.

SEVEN

Wedding Bells, Again

Another Mistake

The first thing I did was notify my boss, Jay Rossbach, that I was going to marry Gerry McNamara and move to Phoenix. I was resigning as buyer, and would stay as long as needed to train a replacement. He was absolutely shocked.

"Of course I'm happy for you," he said, "but what a surprise. Let me digest this, and I'll get back to you. Meanwhile, let's go in and tell Adam Gimbel and Ray Johnson the news." (They were the president and vice-president of the store.) They, too, were sorry to see me leave, but Mr. Gimbel immediately remarked, "What's that McNamara doing stealing our best buyer. He certainly knows a good thing when he sees it!"

As I left their offices, I was reminded of the last time I'd been there. It was about a year ago, when the opening for a merchandise manager's position on my floor became available. It was the next step up from buyer, and I knew I could do a great job. I was ready, having been buyer for ten years, experiencing recognition by top management for outstanding results.

"Mr. Johnson," I said, "I'd like to apply for the merchandise manager's position on the seventh floor. You already know what I've accomplished, and I feel ready for this promotion. I know everyone down there, and have plenty of ideas to help build the other departments like I did my own. Let me summarize for you what I think should be done to improve the entire seventh floor. I've lived with it for over ten years."

He cleared his throat and without hesitating told me, "Ollie, you're the best buyer we have in the store, but we'll never put a woman in as merchandise manager. Women are just too emotional and irrational."

I was stunned! "I can't believe you're saying that, Mr. Johnson, since I've worked ten years in the store and have proved my ability. I doubt anyone has ever reported me as 'emotional' or 'irrational.' Please check around and then get back to me. I'm really interested in this position and I don't want to be written off just because I'm a woman!"

He never did get back to me, but a few days later Larry Rogers, formerly manager of our Springfield, New Jersey store, appeared. He called each buyer into his office, one at a time, to tell us he was the new merchandise manager of the seventh floor.

When I was told, he also added, "Ollie, Mr. Johnson told me about your interest in this position. I'm sorry they didn't give it to you because you're a helluva merchant and know more about merchandising and buying than most of us. But I'm here and I want to work with you and learn from you."

I wanted to scream in frustration, "Work with me? Learn from me? Like Hell you will, because I won't be coming to your office. I should be sitting in your seat. I deserve to be sitting in your seat. Am I a freak of nature just because I was born female!"

Instead, I said, "Mr. Rogers, I'm sorry you were given the job I wanted so desperately." Here I was, eager to do more with my career, yet I couldn't. I had hit the "glass ceiling." Ten years later, we would call this discrimination.

I returned to my office and remembered another episode with top management that had upset me almost as much. It happened about three years before I left Saks. I had been approached by *The Chicago Sun-Times* to write a fashion column that would be distributed through King Features Syndicate. I thought it was a great idea, and I could write it at home in the evening. We called it, "Wright About Fashion," by Ollie Wright. Brochures were printed up and press releases sent out. Within weeks the column was in forty-two newspapers, appearing weekly in many major markets like Chicago, Detroit, Phoenix, San Diego, etc. I wrote the column for about five months. Then, one day I received a call from Mr. Gimbel's office that he wanted to see me immediately. I rushed upstairs and was escorted in by his secretary. He was not in a friendly mood. As I sat down he handed me a newspaper with my fashion column in it.

"Ollie, what is all this about? Nobody around here seems to know."

I could see he was agitated. I calmly replied, "It's a fashion column I've been writing for a few months now."

"Did it ever occur to you to clear this through management?" he asked. "It's a direct conflict of interest and I'm very upset with you. If this is indicative of your loyalty to the store, then consider yourself dismissed!"

"Oops," I thought. "Did I hear him correctly? Am I fired?" Out loud I said, "You can't fire me, Mr. Gimbel. I'm the best buyer you have. You said so yourself." I wondered whether he had read more than the one column.

He continued, "Eddie Bedford (manager of our Detroit store) sent me a few of these articles, and I don't like you giving out information about your buy."

"But, Mr. Gimbel," I interrupted, "every single article is written in generalities: Fall Trends, The New Looks, How to Accessorize with Flair. To me it's like free weekly advertising. I don't agree with you. It adds even more credibility to our fashion leadership. Proof of its popularity is the number of fashion inquiries we get in the mail every week."

Mr. Gimbel paused for a moment, then said, "If you want to keep your job, you will have to stop writing this column. That's all, Ollie. Talk to Jay Rossbach as soon as it's done."

I was not too happy with this ultimatum. I needed my job more than the column, so I stopped in to see Jay Rossbach.

He had already been prepared and in his booming voice said, "Ollie, you'll have to stop writing your column. Contact your people and let me know when it's done."

I went back to my office a little hurt and a lot angry. I called my editor in Chicago and told him the story. He was sorry to end it, but asked if he could run the last three articles I had already submitted and consider it finalized. I said okay and confirmed it when I asked Mr. Rossbach if it was all right. That ended my syndicated column. I wondered whether those two disappointments helped make my decision to leave my job, particularly the promotion I should have had. I never did get over that.

Looking back over those twelve years at Saks, most of my experiences were happy. My department grew substantially over that period, and I was proud to say we never had negative figures. It was quite an accomplishment, evolving an average department to one that was sophisticated and designer-oriented. We began to attract many petite clients to our department because we were the first to carry sizes three and five. The Safinia Collection became the most important part of this success. I had more fun working on it each season, because management gave me complete freedom. After I left they never could find the right person to style the collection so instead management decided to discontinue it, permanently.

Working for Saks Fifth Avenue at that time required travelling to the branch stores, holding staff meetings, and transferring merchandise that was slow selling back to New York. We didn't have computer printouts but worked with big "unit control" books instead. I would play the Safinia persona part of the time and buyer the rest. I never was bored; there wasn't any time for that. The experience I gained doing all this was put to good use in the future.

Once I notified management I was leaving, I knew I was committed. The next project was finding a realtor to handle the sale of my brownstone. Through friends I found a very aggressive, but also likable and friendly, agent. She and I agreed on the price and terms. I wanted all cash. Since I would be living in Arizona, she understood my desire not to carry any paper. Next, I notified my tenants of the pending change of ownership. The biggest job lay ahead: packing and throwing out. Since I was still working at the store, most of this was done evenings and weekends. Gerda was a big help. She decided not to go with us because she had just recently been engaged.

"I will really miss Cindy," she said softly. "I couldn't love her more if she were my own child."

I knew that, because she showed it every day with her tenderness and concern. "And we will miss you, Gerda," I sighed. "She has really had two mothers for the past three years we've been together. I can't begin to thank you for all you have meant to both of us." I really loved Gerda. She was my friend, and when we made the big move she not only packed all of Cindy's things, she also helped with all the rest. When John Wright and I were divorced, she was there for my support, refusing to take any time off herself. She listened to me for months talk about my romance with Gerry McNamara and the long distance ups and downs. Now, with the Big Move to Arizona, she was there helping out with organizing and packing.

Gerry and I decided we should be married in New York before moving to Arizona. The marriage took place at the City Courthouse in New York City March 12, 1965. Witnesses to the marriage were Cathy Apothaker and John Barker Hickox. The Justice of the State Supreme Court performed the ceremony, which lasted about five minutes. I didn't feel at all like a bride, and as I looked around I wished I had a bridal bouquet of pink and peach roses or multicolored tulips to add some color to the place. Everything around us was grey and more grey.

"I would like to fling my invisible bouquet to the next hopeful City Courthouse bride," I thought to myself.

There were several more couples waiting for the big moment, and as we left they smiled at us. It was all very simple: bride, groom, witnesses, Justice of the Peace, paperwork, and, "Now I pronounce you man and wife." My previous marriage to John Wright was somewhat similar. We were married in Amityville, Long Island, simply because it was near Shelter Island where we had a home. A Justice of the Peace performed that ceremony, which was about five minutes long as well. Come to think of it, my first marriage to Judah Holstein was the most "weddingy." It was held in a Catholic

Church, where I marched down the aisle as a bride should. My sister Helen was my maid of honor. My mother flew down from Auburn with Helen, and they were my only family. My mother wasn't too happy about that marriage, because she felt I should wait until Judah returned from Vietnam and decide then. She was right!

These thoughts raced through my head as Cathy, Gerry, Barker, and I left the Courthouse. We made plans for a small wedding reception at La Grenouille restaurant that evening, so we had a few hours to ourselves. Gerry and I checked into the Plaza Hotel for the evening and sank into wedded bliss. A few hours later, we met everyone at the restaurant at eight o'clock. Refreshed and dressed in my new azure blue silk suit, I was happy to see that our group had all arrived. We drank champagne, made a few toasts, and by the end of the meal we were all a little bubbly and fizzy. There was a special wedding cake ordered, just the right size for ten of us, that was all white on the outside and chocolate inside. Two of my closest friends, Vera and Arthur, who owned a dress firm on Seventh Avenue, kept saying how much they were going to miss me. Gerry couldn't stop telling us, "I'm the lucky one here and have to pinch myself to make sure it's true." And I was the happy bride, looking forward to a new life in Phoenix, Arizona.

A few days before the wedding, a farewell party was held for me at the store. I was very touched, because so many of my friends were there, including Adam Gimbel and Ray Johnson. Jay Rossbach made a moving speech and presented me with a beautiful sterling silver tray that had all signatures of those present engraved on it. To this day I still cherish that tray. I worked at the store only two more days, having trained my replacement, and went from floor to floor to say my farewells. Lots of hugs and tears later, I packed up what was left of "me" in the office and departed for the last time.

In the taxi going home, I couldn't help reminiscing about my almost twelve years at Saks Fifth Avenue as buyer of department 701. Years later I would appreciate even more how much I had learned in that position, much of it self-taught because I had no one to teach me. The job was my teacher. My antennae were on constant alert, absorbing knowledge, developing taste, organizing the "Buy," planning, projecting, analyzing, and taking chances. I learned early on never to play it too safe because "safe can be dumb." I also discovered that "you're only as good as your last Buy." That can be very humbling. Important in my learning process was the simple statement, "you need the manufacturer as much as he needs you." I never forgot that. Don't be a "know it all." Appreciate. Compliment. Say thank you. Teach by example. Develop a positive attitude. Ask questions. Yes, I learned a lot on the job, and I made full use of it when we opened our own store eleven years later.

EIGHT

The Valley of the Sun

Life in Phoenix, Arizona

The next two weeks were spent packing. Gerry had returned to Phoenix to prepare the house for our arrival. The day of departure finally arrived, and Cindy and I boarded the plane for Phoenix. She was so excited–she had never been on a plane before—and was full of questions. The stewardess brought her up to the cockpit to meet the pilot, who showed Cindy the instrument panels. That was the highlight of her flight.

After five hours, we were ready to descend into the Phoenix airport, and Cindy, with her nose pressed to the window, exclaimed, "Mommy, look, the buildings are getting bigger and bigger!"

When we arrived, Gerry was there to meet us at the gate. After hugs and kisses and collecting our luggage, we were on the way to our new home. It was only a twenty minute drive, a convenience that came in handy as the years went by. The house was located on East Georgia, a side street off Twentieth Street, opposite the Biltmore Hotel property. It was a corner plot, about two acres of land. I later found out we were part of the Bartlett Estates, which was a residential area with horse privileges. The driveway was gravel with a center round planter filled with desert foliage. As we approached the front door, I could sense Gerry was a little nervous, wondering what I thought of the place. As I walked inside, all I could think of was how much fun (and work) it was going to be to transform it all. Gerry informed me the house had been designed by Blaine Drake, one of Frank Lloyd Wright's students. Typical of Wright's taste, the floors were bare concrete with inside planters along one wall in the living room. All walls were cold, grey, exposed concrete block. The living room and dining room were like one room, with plate glass windows overlooking the outer patio. The ceilings were low, about eight to nine feet high. The kitchen really needed work, but it had a nice skylight that let in the sunlight. A long, narrow hallway led to the bedrooms. Connected to the main part of the house was a large two room addition that could be entered only from the outside. One room was a family playroom and the other was used as a workshop by the previous owner, Jerry Colpitts. (We were told he had committed suicide in the workshop, and his wife, Marjorie, immediately put the house up for sale. She was devastated.) There was also a separate little house, complete with bathroom and shower, used as a cabana. It was located near the kitchen.

I turned to Gerry and said, "I love the house and can't wait to get started on it!"

"I know," he replied, "I feel the same way."

Our new life in Phoenix began. Gerry went to work at Saks Fifth Avenue every morning, including Saturday, and I stayed at home with Cindy. The first few weeks were filled with unpacking and organizing. All my furniture and possessions arrived on schedule and were placed in various rooms. We decided our first project would be tiling the entire floor area throughout the house. No small task. Gerry himself jack-hammered the cement floors to prepare them for the tile men. Night after night he would eat dinner and then go to work with the rat-a-tat-tat terrible noise. When it was finally done weeks later, our beautiful pale green tile was installed by the tile men. We ripped out all the indoor planters, which increased the size of the room, and transformed the whole area. I had managed to salvage five beautiful old doors from the Myron Taylor mansion, and all five were installed in our new home. Also, we replaced the plate glass windows on two walls of the dining room with ceiling-to–floor, antique, leaded glass, paned windows overlooking the outdoor patio. We did the same in the three bedrooms. All walls were stuccoed off-white, finally eliminating the prison-grey, cold, dreary

Cindy in the first grade at the Montessori school

look. While this was going on inside, the outside gravel driveway was blacktopped and the center desert planting eliminated. In its place, we installed a beautiful stone fountain and surrounded the circular base with a two-foot flower bed.

During these projects, I experienced my first two summers of endless desert heat. We decided to put a twenty-by-forty swimming pool inside the enclosed patio, and over the years, it turned out to be the most used area of the house. Cindy loved it, so we hired a swimming instructor to teach her how to swim. When she turned four, we put her in morning nursery school, and later we learned about a new school for children four to twelve called The Arizona Language School. The instructor believed in teaching very young children foreign languages in addition to the normal curriculum. We enrolled Cindy, and before long she was learning Russian, French, and Spanish. We were thrilled, and Cindy loved it. Every morning she was required to greet the instructor in Russian. We projected that in four years she would be fluent in three languages. Then, unfortunately, the teacher was ordered to close the school because of some bureaucratic rules. All the parents together couldn't win the fight. So, at age five, Cindy was put into the first grade at public grade school. "Mommy," she wondered, "why did they close my school? I liked it and so did my friends." None of us could adequately answer that question.

During those months I was kept very busy, overseeing the house renovation, and taking care of Cindy. Then, out of nowhere, I received a phone call from the Women's Page Editor of the Phoenix Republic and Gazette newspaper. She had learned that I was the person responsible for the "Wright about Fashion" column that had appeared in their paper weekly a few years before.

"Ollie," she asked, "How would you like to write a similar column again, just for our paper?"

I wasn't sure and replied, "Let me think about it for a few days and I'll call you."

"All right," she said, "but let me tell you how much our readers loved your column. We'll work out details to make it easy for you."

That evening I talked to Gerry about the offer, and he was thrilled. "Honey, I think it would be wonderful and think you should do it!"

I called Reba the following day and accepted. We decided to name the column "Right About Fashion" by Ollie McNamara. I submitted my first few columns, and before long I was asked to do a four-page fashion spread as a seasonal, extended fashion column. It involved selecting the fashions to be photographed, hiring the models and photographer, doing the layout, and writing the fashion story. It was time-consuming, challenging, and rewarding. I did this mornings, so I could spend the afternoons with Cindy. Her first grade class was out at two-thirty, and I would always pick her up. We would then do little errands, play "tea with her Barbie dolls," or visit Saks to say hello to Gerry. She soon became the store "pet." I, meanwhile, received another phone call from Reba at the newspaper.

"Could you possibly write two columns a week instead of one?" she asked. "We have had enormous response to your column, and my editor was anxious to add to it."

"Oh, Reba," I don't think I need another deadline at this point," I wailed. "I'd be willing to do two, or even three, special four page spreads a year but not two columns each week."

"Okay," she said, "I'll get back to you."

She called the next day, and confirmed three of the four page fashion spreads a year plus the weekly fashion column. I thought for a moment and realized I was getting tempted right into a local career, but it was nice added income. Since Gerry's divorce, half his salary went for alimony and child support, and the rest for household expenses. All additions and alterations on the house were paid for by me from proceeds of the brownstone house sale. The renovation took years. We re-fenced the huge pasture, landscaped all areas, planted lawns, built stables for Gerry's horses, connected the work-shop-family room to the main house, raised and extended walls around the entire house, completely tiled the cabana, and replaced the windows there. Like all homes, it was never-ending.

In the midst of all this, I became pregnant. Since Gerry already had two daughters and I had one, we really wanted a boy. I'll never forget the evening of February 23. 1967. Gerry and I were at the Heart Ball held at the Biltmore Hotel. I was wearing a hot pink, empire-waisted, taffeta gown. The bodice was all beaded. You could hardly tell I was pregnant, but I felt like a balloon. At about ten-thirty, as I was walking to the bathroom, I knew something was going to happen. My water was about to break. I was gently guided into the bathroom, and Gerry came running in a few minutes later.

"Are you all right? What happened?" He was frantic!

"You'd better rush me to the hospital." I said, "I think I'm about to give birth."

"Oh, my God," his voice was louder. "Wait here while I get the car."

By now I felt like I was going to be tomorrow's headlines. I was surrounded by a group of women, all giving me advice. "Hold it in," they said, " You can do it. You can do it." Gerry returned in minutes, having asked the parking attendant to bring our car to the entrance. Fortunately, we lived just around the corner, and we made it home just in time. I changed my clothes, and we rushed to St. Joseph's Hospital. At 3:13 a.m. on February 24, 1967, James Patrick McNamara was born. He weighed six pounds, eleven ounces. Two days later we brought him home. We had already prepared a room for him adjacent to our bedroom with a bassinet and baby blue everything. Cindy was fascinated by her tiny, new brother and immediately wanted to hold him. At that point, it was love at first sight. James (we called him Jamie then) was not an easy baby. He cried a lot and let us know he liked to be held. I

James on his first birthday. He loved ice cream

Jamie, two years old, taking apart our telephone and putting it back together again

didn't breast feed either of my two children, which helped keep me mobile. Jamie loved his little bottle of formula, and within six months was a happy, growing boy. Luckily, we had found a wonderful nanny for James when he was born. Mrs. Iffland only worked with infants, and took care of Jamie until he reached the age of two. She was kind and loving, the motherly type, heavy set, and bosomy. She was a big help to us, and we continued to use her for baby-sitting whenever she was able, particularly on Sundays when Gerry played polo.

Since Gerry worked six days a week, Sunday was his one day off. Every single Sunday we would all go to the polo grounds. Nancy, Gerry's twelve-year-old daughter, spent the day with us Sunday after Sunday after Sunday. She helped her Dad load the horse trailer with his two polo ponies and would hot-walk them during the games. I resented her at first, because she was always around on the one day I wanted to spend with Gerry. It soon became obvious that Sundays alone with Gerry would never happen. As I look back on it now, I guess it was selfish on my part to ask for even one Sunday alone with him. The resentment grew on her part as well as mine. I made very little effort to befriend her, but she was very sweet to Cindy. Nancy always had a weight problem and with her pudgy body and rosy cheeks was a pre-teen who needed help. It was obvious she didn't like me any more than I liked her. I think she held me responsible for the breakup of her parents' marriage. Her sister, Joan, was hardly ever around. She eventually moved to Hawaii, had two children, and moved back to the States. When Nancy was in her teens, she used to baby sit Cindy. They became good friends at that time.

It was now 1967. Gerry and I had been married for almost two years. Cindy was six years old, and it was time to think seriously about her heart problem. It was always there, an underlying worry drifting in and out of my consciousness. Cindy appeared to be so normal, full of life and enthusiasm, it didn't seem possible she needed this very intricate surgery. We searched for, and found, a highly qualified heart specialist in Phoenix, Dr. Lee Ehrlich. He examined Cindy thoroughly and agreed with the doctors in New York that she needed the operation. He recommended her open heart surgery be done by Dr. Denton Cooley at Children's Hospital in Houston, Texas. He was trained by Dr. DeBakey, one of the finest heart surgeons of the time and among the first to do heart transplants. It was agonizing for me to think of Cindy's little body undergoing surgery, but I was grateful her condition was operable. Arrangements were made between the doctors and me for the summer after Cindy's sixth birthday, in 1967. The months flew by quickly, and when it was time to leave, Cindy was incredibly brave, never crying, never complaining. She and I flew to Houston together. Gerry stayed behind. I never dreamed he wouldn't be there, particularly during surgery. I never said a word, but I really needed him with me at that time.

When we arrived, I checked into the hotel, and that afternoon Cindy was admitted into the hospital. We talked about her upcoming operation, and she instinctively understood how important it was. Dr. Cooley visited us early that evening, with his entourage of doctor-trainees following him from room to room in total awe, a little like Jesus and His Disciples.

He asked if there was anything he could do for us, and I replied hopefully, "could you please do Cindy's surgery first?"

He said he would try. Very early the next morning, we were advised we were first on his operating list. Dr. Cooley had switched his schedule around to do that. I was so grateful. I had been told a few weeks before by Dr. Ehrlich in Phoenix, that when Cindy was born, open-heart surgery offered only a forty percent chance of survival. It took twenty-four hours to clean a non-disposable machine after each surgery. Now, six years later, they used a disposable heart-lung machine that was thrown out after each operation. Dr. Cooley performed eleven operations the day Cindy had hers. He did none of the initial cutting into the body and sewing up afterwards. He concentrated on doing "perfect judgment" work. In Cindy's case, he widened the pulmonary outflow tract and scraped out the membranous material lining it. How much he removed was a very delicate decision. She also had a quarter-sized hole between the lower two chambers of her heart. Dr. Cooley patched up the hole with a Dacron patch. Cindy's surgery started at seven a.m. and I didn't hear anything until two in the afternoon.

All the parents of children undergoing surgery that day were together in one large waiting room. We shared experiences. We wept. We hugged. And, in our own silent worlds, we prayed for a positive outcome. During the nine hours I waited, one infant from South Africa died during surgery. It was heart-wrenching to watch the mother sob over her lost baby. Another child came through the surgery but died afterwards due to shock to his system. We were all part of each sorrow. Little children were dying of cancer. One little boy had already had one kidney removed and his second about to be removed. It was all very sad, and memories of the experience still linger.

When you sit there in the waiting room filled with parents whose children are scheduled for serious surgery, all you can think of is God, merciful God, help my child. Prayer is all we have left. "Please, dear God, let her surgery be successful," I pleaded silently. Each one of us was immersed in our own pain, and when a child died, we were all struck down. We knew ours could be next. I learned, many years later, the concept of acceptance, and until I knew Cindy was alive after surgery, I couldn't bear to think of her dying. Once again God was good to me and spared me that agony. The only way any of the mothers could bear the pain of loss was to accept it and go on. That took great inner strength and God to lean on.

Finally, seven hours later, Dr. Cooley came down the hallway towards the waiting room. I was frozen with fear for the worst. He told me Cindy had come through the operation successfully but the next twenty-four hours were critical. I threw my arms around the doctor in such relief I could hardly speak. She was in intensive care, and I was able to see her once they shrouded me in a clean white garment and a face mask. When I walked into the room and saw her, I was momentarily shocked. She was in an oxygen tent and had so many tubes and machines around, you could hardly see her thin, little body. Her eyes were closed, and as I stood there she slowly opened them and gave me a wan, little smile. My heart leapt. She was alive; she had come through the surgery! "Oh, how I love you, Cindy!" I was permitted to visit her regularly for the next few days until she was strong enough to be released from the intensive care unit and put into her own private room. I was also allowed to stay and sleep in Cindy's room in a separate bed provided for parents.

To be able to stay in the hospital with her until she was released was an added feature provided by Texas Children's Hospital. I was with her day and night until two weeks later when we were told Cindy was strong enough to go home. As we wheeled Cindy out I remembered the many times we went up and down, up and down, those corridors in her wheelchair. We said goodbye to all our new friends, the doctors, nurses, and patients. Cindy was holding a little, heart-shaped pillow given to every child who survives at Texas Children's Hospital. She was now a permanent member of the Heart Club. The pillow had a little tear in it as if the heart had been broken and repaired with little stitches. The motto stitched on it read, "It's great to be alive, and help others." You're very conscious of that after your child survives.

This experience made me realize how fragile human life is and how miraculous open heart surgery can be. I look at Cindy today, my miracle baby brimming with the fullness and goodness of life, and am full of gratitude for her chance to Be. For years afterwards, I worked on the Heart Ball committee and annually did a huge fashion show to raise funds. It was one small way to say thank you.

It had been almost three weeks since we left Phoenix, and Gerry was happy to see us home again. We put Cindy to bed immediately because she

Cindy in high school. She was quite a good rider by then.

was tired, and I couldn't wait to pick up little Jamie, napping away, to give him hugs and kisses. I had missed him desperately during those three weeks. Gerry too. We sat and talked until Jamie awakened, and when we heard his familiar, "wahhhhh," I swooped him up in my arms. I think Jamie wondered who I was for a moment until a big smile replaced his welcome wail. "Mommy's home," I said, and gave him my three weeks of missed hugs and kisses. Mrs. Iffland was eager to tell me all about Jamie's progress over the time we had been gone. Gerry decided to go back to Saks until closing time, so Mrs. Iffland and I had a cup of tea and talked and talked. I wanted to hear everything.

Now that Jamie was six months old, he was beginning to develop his own personality. He was lovable and sweet one minute, demanding and difficult the next. He would scream for attention from his crib, throwing out his toys and bottle on the floor. He was angry and impatient if he didn't get his own way NOW. Often he would stand up in his crib, tiny hands clutching the top and "Wahhhhh. Wahhhhh" until he was picked up and

⑯ 1971 Resolutions for Jamie

① I will not use dirty words.
② I will act nice at the table
③ I will eat everything on my plate
④ I will not get up once I'm tucked in bed
⑤ I will not rebel against my parents
⑥ I will not hit the dog.
⑦ I will not throw stones while Cindy is riding the horse
⑧ I will treat other people's property with respect
⑨ I will not litter.
⑩ I will be nice to baby sitters.

⑪ I will not break things,
⑫ I will be nice at breakfast
⑬ I will obey my parents
⑭ I will not things the without permission
⑮ I will not throw silverware.

Jamie's "New Year's Resolutions," when he was four years old.

cuddled by me. Mrs. Iffland warned me not to pick him up every time, because he would continue the behavior knowing I would give in. We learned early on Jamie was going to be a handful. He had a mind of his own, and by the time he was three, we knew he needed professional help. He was diagnosed hyperactive, with attention deficit disorder, ADD. The doctors prescribed Ritalin, but we both agreed not to put him on medication. We coped, hoping he might slow down his perpetual motion and outgrow his constant chatter. When we couldn't quiet him down to listen to us, we nicknamed him "Motor Mouth." Accurate, but not too kind. Jamie was a gifted child, curious, and eager to learn. He amazed all of us when, at age two, he took apart our telephone and then put it back together again. There were numerous examples of his advanced abilities. There were also examples of his anger when he didn't get his own way. He would scream, throw things, and want constant attention. He was happiest when totally engrossed in a project, beginning in his playpen with building blocks and later on the floor with his erector sets.

Jamie was only seven-months-old when Cindy returned home from her open-heart surgery in Houston. It took many months to regain her strength and return to school. She was very happy to be back and able to catch up with the missed work. I stayed home with the children until James entered kindergarten. Gerry and I were very busy socially during this period, entertaining visiting New York buyers and executives. We always took them out to dinner, starting off with drinks at home and then off to Trader Vic's or Chez Louis for dinner. We also entertained at home with dinner parties or large cocktail parties when a visiting designer arrived. We had one of these larger parties for Oscar de la Renta and his wife, Francoise. He was very charming; she was very French. When Bill Blass visited, we had a huge party, because everyone wanted to meet him. He was very handsome, witty, and debonair. He stayed over a few extra days, and we became good friends. There was always a big fashion show the day after these introductory parties. In season (January through April) there was an endless stream of designers visiting us from New York. There were all the other social events as well: The Heart Ball, The Symphony Ball, The Cancer Ball, etc. Private parties and fund raising events were frequent, and we met many interesting people. But something was not right.

One thing I had noticed over the past year was how much more Gerry was drinking. He would turn into an angry, red-faced, other person and suddenly start screaming.

"I can't take this any longer. I can't stand living like this. I wish I were dead. Dead! Dead! Dead!"

We never knew what triggered those rages, but when he started to drink at lunch, before dinner, and during dinner, we were always afraid. We knew one of two things would happen. He would either leave the table and pass out on the couch in the family room or he would start a fight. This happened night after night after night. Many evenings he would be very angry at James for not eating, and he would scream and belittle him at the table. He would try to force him to eat, and James would throw up on his plate. I begged Gerry to leave the table and I would sit with James until he finished his meal. One evening Gerry was so angry he went to James' room, ripped his computer out of the wall, and removed it from his room. That sickened me, but devastated James. He didn't think he'd ever see his computer again. The next morning Gerry returned it to James as though nothing had happened. He didn't remember a thing, but I suddenly realized this was the beginning of his blackouts.

As manager of Saks Fifth Avenue, Phoenix, from 1965 to 1975, Gerry was responsible for the success of the store. He always looked for capable people with enthusiasm. As a result, year after year, the Phoenix store had the biggest increases in the chain. He was described as a maverick, doing things not done by the other stores. This irritated top management in New York. Gerry was an artist at heart and liked color. When directives from New York told out-of-town stores to keep colors neutral, Gerry would not change the colorful painted walls where clothes were hung. He was convinced color made the store look exciting. And it did. He painted the walls and insides of bins where clothes were hung bright red, blue, and orange. Everybody loved it and responded to it with increased sales. The New York store wanted a consistent look throughout the chain. If you visited any of the Saks stores throughout the country, you would recognize the similarities. Everything was bland off-white. The Phoenix store was unique, and that was exactly what New York management did not want.

A perfect example of this happened in the early 1970s. Cindy and James were in school all day, and I was free to do whatever I wanted. Gerry had just lost the manager of his designer departments and asked me to help. Since I had been a buyer for Saks in New York, management was happy I was willing to do it. They also gave me my own department with a limited budget to spend. Little by little the department grew. At this time we were planning our summer vacation and decided to drive to northern Arizona. I had never seen that part of the state. We stopped at little towns along the way, and I began to notice shops that carried jewelry made by the Indians. I became very excited, because I had never seen anything like it before.

"Gerry, look at this spectacular Indian jewelry! We should buy some pieces for the store, and I'll show them in the next fashion show we have."

He looked at me in shock and said, "Ollie, the broomstick skirt and Indian squash blossom necklace phase is finished. Nobody wants that anymore."

I persisted. "I'd like to update it and show the jewelry with designer dresses and flowy at-home clothes. I know it will look stunning."

I pushed him to buy a few pieces, and he finally did. We selected a small assortment of necklaces, bracelets, and belts.

Little did we know at the time what we were starting. Nobody was wearing, thinking, or talking about Indian jewelry. We knew nothing about the craft, the artistry, the value of truly fine pieces. I was approaching all of this from a fashion point of view with my instinctive taste and eye at work. I started to wear the jewelry in the store and out socially. People commented on the belt or the necklace and asked where they could buy them. We sold out of everything within a few weeks. Gerry was amazed. He called New York to explain what was happening and requested a special budget in order to purchase more. I think they thought we were crazy, but the sales told the real story.

Gerry now needed to visit the Indians on the reservations and return to the people we had purchased from initially. He also sought out a number of trading posts. In time, he became very knowledgeable. As he took these short buying trips, I asked one of my knitwear vendors if she could make some special hand-loomed knits to wear with Indian jewelry. I wanted to use adaptations of Navajo rug patterns as borders that worked with the jewelry. We only used black, white, and beige in order to highlight the multi-colored borders. When the pieces were finished, we were very excited and contacted Joe Stacey, editor of *Arizona High-ways*, to come to the store to see a fashion show of the collection. He was curious to see what a high-fashion store like Saks Fifth

Avenue would do. With each outfit, we massed Indian jewelry around the necklines, used concho belts in silver and turquoise, and added matching bracelets and earrings where needed. They looked sensational!

Joe was very excited about the concept and said, "We're doing a special *Arizona Highways* Hall of Fame issue on Indian jewelry, and we're nearing our deadline. I want to use every one of these garments in that magazine. Can you photograph them on time?"

"We can do it; I know we can," I promised enthusiastically.

After booking the models and arranging for the magazine's photographer, we were up at dawn the following day photographing. The pictures turned out to be spectacular, and Joe used every one of them in the August, 1974 issue of *Arizona Highways*.

It was the first time the magazine had ever shown fashion in its pages. Photographs of our hand-loomed knits, laden with Indian jewelry, were scattered throughout the issue amongst the incredible jewelry featured by *Arizona Highways*. We had no idea the impact they would make. As the days went by, we started receiving phone calls and letters of inquiry. As the magazine reached its more distant readers, we were deluged with countless orders from all fifty states and six foreign countries. Our customers were thrilled to find the perfect dress or pants outfit with a truly Southwestern flavor to wear with their important Indian jewelry. One woman from Florida ordered seven outfits.

She had an Indian store and said, "I will now have a different outfit to wear with my Indian jewelry every day of the week." We were amazed.

Then the "trouble" began. All Saks stores from New York, Chicago, Beverly Hills, Detroit, San Francisco, etc. were receiving calls and orders for the clothes and had no idea what was going on. Top management in New York called Gerry to find out "what the Hell this was all about."

"McNamara, are you up to your old tricks again, doing things without New York's permission?"

Instead of, "Thank God, we have a creative manager who knows instinctively when a good thing is happening and acts on it," he heard nothing but complaints. We had created a monster with no idea it would be so successful. Our sales soared to over six figures and kept growing. It couldn't happen. But it did. New York buyers were sent to Arizona, and Gerry took them to Indian reservations. Soon the jewelry was in New York and many of the Saks branch stores. *Vogue* and *Bazaar* did articles. It became a national story.

In order to stay ahead, we planned a new group of knits with authentic designs from ancient Apache baskets. They were photographed against Southwestern backgrounds and used in a brochure mailed to all our customers. Again, response was overwhelming. It took about two years before the Indian jewelry craze subsided and returned to the traders of "collector's quality" pieces. As a result of these experiences, I learned to appreciate the delicacy and beauty of a Leekya or Tsikewa fetish necklace or one of Charles Loloma's bold, modern bracelets. I enjoyed wearing a silver concha belt with grey flannel pants or large graduated silver beads with a cashmere sweater. Today, Ralph Lauren is showing beautiful turquoise and silver jewelry and belts with his collections, making Indian jewelry desirable and high fashion once again. I would still be wearing pieces from my beautiful collection of jewelry and belts if a frightening, and traumatic, event had never occurred.

NINE

The Holdup

Terror in Our House

It was December 28, 1976. We had house guests from Philadelphia visiting us, and Cathy and I were in the kitchen preparing dinner. It was about seven o'clock. Cindy was at church with a girlfriend. Cathy's young daughter, Helena, was in the cabana, and Gerry and Jonathan (Cathy's young son) were in the workshop. Gerry later told us, as he walked out of the workshop to return to the kitchen, that a man wearing a ski mask stepped up and pointed a long-barreled .38 caliber revolver at his head. He said, "cooperate or you'll get it." As the kitchen door swung open, Gerry and Jonathan were rushed through by three men with a gun on the back of Gerry's head.

"Where's the safe?" they kept asking.

"We don't have a safe," Gerry replied.

Momentarily, I thought they were kidding and asked, "Is this a joke?

"This is no joke," snarled one of the men, "get in front of the boy and move into the next room."

They all wore head coverings. As we shuffled into the living room, one of the men ran to the back of the house while the other two covered us with their guns. "Sit down," they ordered. As we sat there, James asked what kind of gun the man had. He was ignored. At that moment, Helena walked in oblivious to what was going on.

"What's happening?" she asked.

"Get over with the rest of them and sit down," he answered.

He sounded angry that she had appeared out of nowhere. The man who ran to the back reappeared with two other men whose faces were covered with panty hose. He had gone back to let them in through the locked door. There were a total of five men. Gerry was lying down, quivering wildly, as though he were having a heart attack. They tied our hands and taped our mouths. We were terrified they were going to shoot us all. Three men returned to the back of the house, ending up with pillow cases full of all my jewelry, Indian pots, and anything else of value. When they came up front, they continued ransacking, taking all my beautiful silver and whatever else they felt was valuable. When they were finished, they led us back to the bathroom, taped our arms and legs and tied the door so we couldn't leave. By now we were really frightened. We were certain they were going to shoot each one of us, lying there on the floor, before they left. When they were gone, James found his pocketknife and was able to cut himself free. He then helped free the rest of us. We were very quiet, not knowing whether the robbers were still in the house. After about five minutes, James and his father stepped out and walked down the hall. The men were gone. We went outside to find they had driven off in our vintage Cadillac station wagon, and had slashed all four tires of our Mercedes so we couldn't pursue them. We then called the police and waited.

"I wonder why Otto (our dog) didn't bark," said James.

He then ran to the back of the house to find Otto lying unconscious inside his dog run. He had obviously been poisoned and was sick for a week. James turned out to be the hero, and we were very proud of him.

When the police finally arrived, we gave them a complete report. We could give no facial descriptions because of the masks. Cindy returned home after all this was over and was shocked to hear the story. She was happy to have missed it all. The next day our station wagon was found in the parking lot of the Cine Capri theater just around the corner from out house. We picked it up, fortunately undamaged, and drove it home.

As we reviewed the entire episode and tried to remember everything that was taken, we could only say we were happy to be alive. They stole my entire collection of priceless Indian jewelry, which I miss even today. The worst part was the invasion of privacy and the anger that followed. The police never found the men, nor did we ever retrieve any of the stolen pieces.

Although it was one of our most devastating experiences, something equally difficult happened about a year before. Gerry was called to New York for the annual managers' meeting and received compliments from top management for his excellent sales and profit picture for the year.

He sensed a "guarded" tone he couldn't explain and called me that evening to say, "Ollie, something's up. I can't put my finger on it but they're not acting very friendly."

I tried to reassure him with "probably just a bad moment that has nothing to do with you at all." When he returned to Phoenix a few days later he was sure something was going on. This was confirmed a week later when one of the New York management team came to Phoenix. He was to meet with Gerry in his office the following morning.

That evening Gerry kept saying over and over, "Why would Elliot visit me a week after I had just been in New York? They have something up their sleeves. Do they want to transfer me? They gave me a glowing report." He was really worried, and tomorrow couldn't come soon enough.

Gerry arrived early at the store the following morning. He was very nervous when he left home not knowing what to expect.

"Please call me when you're finished," I said, "I'd like to know what happens." As he left, I sensed a big lump in my throat, fearful of change and the unknown.

We never expected what Elliot had to say. He appeared to be nervous and not too happy. As he shuffled some papers on the desk, he looked directly at Gerry and said, "Gerry, you've done a great job running this store and management considers Phoenix the most successful in the chain. However, we find you're difficult to handle at times because of your single-minded attitude and strong opinions.

You treat this store as though it were your own and disregard many of the memos from New York. Frankly, we're fed up with your inability to conform and have decided your services are no longer desired. Effective immediately, you are dismissed from your position as manager of the Phoenix store."

Gerry was dumbfounded. He had been with Saks for ten years and never dreamed this would happen.

Elliot added, "We have made arrangements for the new manager to arrive tomorrow, and would appreciate your clearing out the office and removing all your personal belongings by the end of the day." Elliot said he would be in the store until Gerry left...and would he kindly give him the keys before leaving?

That was it. Gerry called to give me the news and said he would be home shortly. He sounded very upset but didn't want to discuss it on the telephone. About two hours later he arrived home, disconsolate and confused. After emptying the car, we sat down and talked.

"Why?" he kept repeating. "What did I do?"

We talked for hours, but nothing was resolved. It was finished. Gerry was a manager who needed more independence because he was so creative. Saks wanted conformists. Maybe that was part of the reason he was fired. He had confrontations with many of the New York buyers and complained, criticized, and antagonized them. He was right in many ways, but he was too blunt, particularly when he told them they weren't sending Phoenix the right kind of merchandise. That didn't matter now because he was unemployed. From day one he was depressed and felt sorry for himself. He would stay in bed all day or walk around in his pajamas. He was very bitter and angry. I tried to talk to him, but he was so wrapped up in himself it was difficult to communicate. He drank all day. "What else is there?" he would remark. "You have your new, exciting job in Italy and I'm left to take care of the children."

Six months before, I had resigned from Saks to join Marina Ferrari in Milan. She was Oleg Cassini's niece, and she was developing a new collection for United States distribution. She wanted me to help design the line with her and later introduce and sell it. This

Grand front entry doors to Capriccio purchased from Lloyds of London

Capriccio ..... the dream boutique of Ollie and Gerry McNamara will celebrate the opening of their new store in the Borgata of Scottsdale MONDAY, NOVEMBER 2 .

.....golden niches and 17th century doors from the Loire.

...leaded Conservatory Windows from Staffordshire.

Throughout the store, we've created a wonderful, warm home, waiting for you and your friends....

6166 N. Scottsdale Road, Scottsdale, Arizona 85251 (602) 991-1900

We sent this brochure to our entire mailing list announcing the opening of Capriccio at the Borgata on November 2, 1981

Join us during the day and enjoy the unique palazzo-like surroundings, overflowing with antiques, paintings, sculptures, and as in our former store... the most beautiful women's clothing in the world. Enter the grand portals from the original Lloyds of London and see.....

.....our Carrara fountain from Florence.

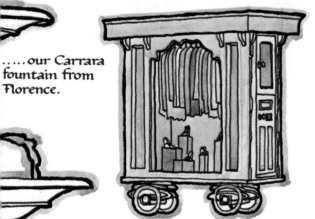

..... an 1860 grocery cart, massive iron gates.
..... our mid-19th century pine-panelled sportswear area and our old English pubs.

.....12 of the largest and most feminine fitting rooms -- antiques and European wall coverings.

864 Prospect Street, La Jolla, California 92037 (714) 459-4189

Barbara Hagerty selling balloons with prize inserts at Capriccio's 20th anniversary party at the Borgata of Scottsdale

Ollie commentating the fashion show at Capriccio's 20th anniversary party

Models ended the fashion show with spectacular beaded evening gowns

Cindy and Grant Jones (Ollie's daughter and son-in-law) with Ollie and Peter at the Capriccio anniversary party

Cindy, James, Ollie, and Gerry McNamara during happier days

Ollie and James at the gala opening of Capriccio, La Jolla, in our new building. the store was downstairs and our private apartment upstairs

The promotion of authentic American Indian jewelry was a huge success. We designed several knitwear groups using traditional Navajo Indian rug patterns and Indian pottery designs as borders

Cindy, James, and me, sitting in front of the antique leaded-glass windows in Cindy's bedroom

Cindy with her cat, BALZAC

James in his red sweater

PERSONAL *Style*

An English coziness, a "slipcover feeling," as Pat Hasbrook describes it, was achieved not only in the choice of fabrics but in the large-scale ("ploopy," says Ollie) upholstery style. Hasbrook's trademark design style of mixing patterns shows to best advantage here. The coffee table ottoman, of two different tapestries with silk bouillon fringe, centers the living room. To the right is a rare velvet and gilt Italian slipper box.

The living room in Phoenix

At Home With Ollie McNamara, the Southwest's Fashion Tastemaker

BY MANYA WINSTED

PHOTOGRAPHY BY LYDIA CUTTER, CUTTER/SMITH

Master bedroom sleeping area

James' bedroom, with unique carved "ceiling" bed

Living room in the La Jolla home with a beautiful coromandel screen behind the floral couch

Celebrating Ollie's birthday with her best friend,
Megan Pierre

Dining room with 18th-century table and high-back chairs

Country kitchen with still-life paintings and open shelves filled with decorative serving pieces

One of my favorite ads at Capriccio featuring a Patricia Lester silk pleated evening gown in soft peach

Cindy's entire wedding party on a Wyoming ranch

Cindy, Ollie, and Peter on Cindy's wedding day

*Peter's daughter, Carol Luery, with her husband Mike,
daughter Sarah, and son Matthew*

*Peter's daughter, Wendy Wilkinson, with her husband Philip, sons Nicholas and Ryan, and
daughter Chelsea*

Peter and Ollie celebrating their first Christmas together.
After 20 years, we are still living happily ever after

was a wonderful opportunity, because in the back of my mind was opening a store of our own in the future. I would be exposed to the Italian fabric market and buyers of the best stores in the country. Gerry would perk up whenever I mentioned "our future store." It wasn't long, however, before he was approached by I. Magnin to manage their Phoenix store at Biltmore Fashion Park. He felt it was a step down, because it was much smaller than Saks Fifth Avenue. I kept encouraging him. "It doesn't matter, Gerry, because you can manage the store temporarily knowing that long range we intend to open up our own business."

Gerry was feeling useless and lesser than after all those weeks out of work. He decided to accept the position and was asked to begin the following day. It was certainly nice to see him dressed in his business clothes going off to work again. His self-image was everything, and once again he looked forward to a new beginning.

Cindy was now fourteen years old and James was eight. When I left for my next trip to Milan, Cindy was asked to take care of James after school until Gerry came home from work around six o'clock. I have always felt guilty about that. She deserved to be free to participate in her own activities, but she was needed at home and never complained about being the substitute Mom. When I returned from Milan two weeks later, I came with the complete collection ready to sell in New York. That trip was scheduled a week later during market week, and although every good store came in, loved the clothes, and bought the line, I knew I was not going to do this again. The logistics of transporting fourteen huge garment bags on and off the plane, hiring a driver with a station wagon, maneuvering the collection up the elevators at the hotel, removing one hundred badly wrinkled garments, pressing them, and getting ready for the next day's appointments was exhausting. With the help of Maryann, who was one of my favorite models from Phoenix, we managed to get all this done.

TEN

The Hong Kong Express

The Endless Flight Over

After twelve years of buying for Saks Fifth Avenue, I now saw the wholesale selling end of it and concluded I much preferred buying. It reminded me of an earlier episode that happened shortly after moving to Phoenix. I was asked by Lee Wong, a well-to-do Chinese friend, if I would help him develop a clothing line in Hong Kong. It was in the late sixties and very few people were going to the Orient to manufacture clothes at that time. He had a friend there, a tailor with many sewers, who could set up a small factory. It would require my traveling to Hong Kong with sketches, ideas, and knowledge of what I wanted. It sounded interesting, and Gerry and I agreed it had enormous potential. I accepted and was given fifty percent of the business without putting up any money.

Little did I know what awaited me. The trip over was endless, and I was very tired by the time we reached the Peninsula Hotel. There were several messages with instructions for the following morning. I quickly unpacked, lay down on the bed, and fell asleep. I was awakened by the phone ringing.

"Hallo, Meez Ollie, this is L'iu Si Fiu, flend of Mista Wong from Phoenix. It is morning and I not hear from you. You okay?"

He had a high-pitched voice but I understood him. I looked at my watch and it was nine o'clock. We were supposed to meet at eight in the lobby of the hotel.

"Oh, I am so sorry," I blurted, "I'll be right down."

Within minutes I was dressed and on my way down the elevator laden with sketches and notebooks. Standing there by the elevator was this little, round man smiling happily, clutching his two hands in front of him, and bowing his head back and forth.

"Meez Ollie, I am Liu Si Fiu. Come, we eat bleckfist first and then we go to factory." He never stopped smiling. He even ate smiling. I liked him immediately.

When we walked out of the hotel, we were instantly swallowed up by the mobs of people in the streets. Massed humanity was everywhere. Little children sat on concrete curbs eating their meals. Laundry hung from building to building in the alleyways, forming rows of white curves. Little booths were packed with tourist items, and as you passed by they would beckon, "Good boggin, sell cheap, verra good stuff." If you hesitated for a moment they were after you. If you wanted to cross the street, you were swept up by the movement of the crowd and almost lifted and carried to the other side. It was fascinating and might have been a bit scary if I hadn't had Liu Si's sure arm at my elbow pushing me along. We finally arrived at the factory, which turned out to be a small room in a building packed with sewing machines and sewers, row on row. I watched in awe as they zoomed their sewing on the machines. It was almost synchronized. Zoom-zoom-zoooooooom.

"Whose garments are they sewing?" I asked.

"Many customahs," Liu Si replied. "We need work. We look at your sketches, we find fabrics, we make patterns, we sew for you."

"Let's get started," I said, "because we only have two weeks to do it all."

"No ploblem," he assured me. I knew immediately he was my kind of worker.

We went to see fabrics first and purchased five-yard cuts to make samples. I had planned small fabric groups, five samples in each fabric with a total of fifty garments. We used only silk because it was difficult to find silk garments in the American market and we could fill a void. When I saw Liu Si's scissors cut into the fabric for the first time, I was ecstatic. He had made ten patterns overnight ready for cutting, and before the day was finished he had cut all ten samples, which were then ready to be sewn. He was truly a master tailor, beyond any I had known before. The following day he assigned one garment each to the sewers, and by the time two weeks were up, the fifty garments were almost ready. Every day at lunchtime, the only break in the day, each sewer would eat his little bowl of rice and drink his tea right at the sewing machine station. Two days before I was ready to return to the United States, every sewer was working in the factory all day and all night in order to complete the collection. I couldn't believe such desire to work. They had no sleep at all, but they finished every piece we had planned. Liu Si Fiu and I had become good friends over the two weeks, and I couldn't compliment him and his sewers enough. They each giggled, smiled, and bowed as I hugged them, one by one. They knew how important it was to complete the collection, so they were filled with pride.

On the plane going back I reviewed my new Chinese memories, including the night I ate shark's fin soup at a formal seven-course dinner. The soup was considered a big delicacy and was presented in my honor. It was thick, white, and lumpy and when I asked what it was, my stomach and brain collided simultaneously. I couldn't bear to eat it, a shark's fin, all blubbery and rubbery, boiled for hours and hours. The Chinese are very sensitive and I didn't want to offend them, so I sipped the liquiddy part and left the lumps. I was so relieved no one commented on my half-full bowl when it was removed at the end of the course. How polite they were!

I slept for most of the trip back and made notes when I wasn't too groggy. Market week in New York was only a few weeks away, and it was up to me to line up appointments with buyers. I knew most of them personally, so they weren't difficult to reach. I even flew to several of their stores to sell the collection we had put together in Hong Kong. The response was incredible. Just as I had expected, they loved the silk fabrics and commented on how difficult it was to find silk garments anywhere in the market. We sold to every store we approached, and to many new ones as well. After I traveled to New York and returned with the orders, I had an unexpected surprise. All week I had been feeling nauseous and tired. It persisted for days until Gerry insisted I see a doctor.

"Why do I have to see a doctor? I'll feel better soon."

But I didn't get better, and when the doctor finally examined me he announced, "Ollie, you're pregnant and having morning sickness early."

What good news. We were both delighted, but it did complicate future plans regarding a return trip to Hong Kong. Within months I was beginning to show, and the last thing I wanted to experience was another endlessly long trip. We told Lee Wong he would need someone else to continue in my place developing the collection. He was disappointed but knew I wouldn't change my mind at that stage. When James was born on February 24, 1967, I became a full time stay-at-home mom.

I loved it. For the first time I could spend as much time as I liked with my children. We had already hired Mrs. Iffland as nanny when James came home from the hospital. He was a happy, healthy, adorable baby who loved being hugged and kissed. Over the following months we observed how curious he was, how moving mobiles above his crib delighted him, and how soft music from a windup toy brought a smile to his face. I think he enjoyed his baths most of all. He kicked and splashed and played with his little rubber duck, then he was wrapped in a big towel and rub-a-dub dried.

James napped while Cindy and I spent free time together. She was six years old when James was born, and I knew that summer she would have her open heart surgery in Houston. We didn't talk about it until a few days before we left. Instead, we spent hours together after school, playing games, reading, and swimming in the pool. She helped set the table for dinner, and once in awhile we'd play grown-up. She loved hobbling around in my high heels and parading in one of my dresses. I often thanked God for bringing me to Phoenix so I could enjoy all those years with my children. I never once regretted the move, nor did I yearn for my career in New York.

Whenever someone would ask, "Don't you miss New York? Your career? Your friends?" my answer was always the same, "Moving to Phoenix was the best decision I ever made.

ELEVEN

The Beginning of the End

A Bitter Farewell

Having another child shook me out of myself: I could now see what was most important in my life, my family. Had I remained in New York, I would not have had time to spend with Cindy and James. I'd have been too busy bringing work home, traveling to branch stores, talking store business with Gerry. In many ways, my life would have remained on hold because of the persistent pattern of sameness. Regardless of how successful my career was, it had a way of claiming and devouring me. I loved my work and was obsessed with being the best. But at what cost? My romantic life was a mess because I had the crazy notion I needed a man to make my life complete. "If only," I would chant, "If only." The three men I did marry had one thing in common. I married them for the wrong reason. Judah Holstein came into my life by way of some invisible, spiritual source. I was convinced he was sent to me by God. John Wright was a marriage of convenience. Handsome and charming, he beguiled me at a weak moment. Gerry McNamara was like a chameleon. His disposition could change from total sweetness to complete anger in an instant. He showed me sweetness only in the early days of courtship. The Gerry I lived with for twenty-three years was far more complex, a combination of Mr. Jekyll, Mr. Hyde, and Lost Soul.

I never did know who the real Gerry was. In the beginning our relationship was loving and lighthearted. He had a sense of humor that made life with him joyful. Little by little he began to change. Everything seemed to annoy him. He became negative and angry; like a snake shedding its skin nightly, he would come home wrapped up in himself with nothing left over for us. He was not an affectionate man and rarely cuddled, hugged, or kissed me or the kids. At home he was either reading the newspaper or watching television, and it hurt to be rebuffed or ignored by him. I could expect explosions regularly, so I watched carefully, walking on eggshells to avoid any confrontations.

One evening as we were departing for a dinner party, Gerry suddenly turned towards me in the car and screamed. "Why do you always have to irritate me, Ollie? You knew I didn't want to go to this party! I don't like these people, and I don't want to have anything to do with them."

He drove the short distance back home, jumped out of the car, and screamed, "You go to your damn party alone!"

I was completely shocked. A half-hour earlier he was talking about looking forward to seeing these long-time friends. I did go to the party alone, made apologies for Gerry, and the hostess quickly changed place cards. Gerry and I never talked about it again.

Another incident, far more serious, happened a few weeks later. Gerry, Cindy, James, and I were returning home after eating dinner at Trader Vic's, one of our favorite restaurants. Gerry had drunk a little too much, and when he slipped into the driver's seat I suggested maybe I should drive instead. That infuriated him! He turned towards me in the car and, without a word, zoomed out of the parking lot at full speed.

"You don't think I can drive, do you! I'll show you how I can drive." And as he careened from left to right, weaving in and out of traffic at full speed, we three made sure our seat belts were on.

"Please, Gerry, let me drive," I pleaded.

"Shut up and stop your whining. I'm sick of your demeaning me all the time!"

He was really angry. Again I tried to convince him to stop, but this time he screamed, "If you don't shut up, when we get home I'm going to get my pistol and shoot all of you. You drive me crazy. "

I knew he was at a breaking point, so I sat quietly as he ranted and raved. Miraculously, we finally reached home safely.

Gerry jumped out of the car, still screaming, "I'm going to kill you: I'm going to kill you all."

He managed to unlock the kitchen door, and as he ran to our bedroom I knew this could turn into a disaster. He grabbed his gun from the lowest drawer next to the bed, and as he turned to aim the gun at me I was close enough to reach out, grab it from his shaky hand, and run out.

As I passed the children, I yelled to Cindy, "Call 911. Tell them to hurry. It's an emergency."

Gerry was close behind me, but I managed to rush out, throw the gun into one of our garbage cans, and continue down the driveway. He didn't see me do that and continued to scream, "I'll get you. I'll get you, you bitch. Give me my gun. Where is my gun?"

As he lunged for me, grabbing my dress, the police sirens could be heard. "Oh, thank God, thank God," I said to myself.

Within minutes the policemen forced Gerry into the house, had him lay on the floor, and asked me, "Do you want to press charges against him?" I looked at this pitiful figure, and somehow knew the worst was over.

"No, I don't think so," I replied. "I think he'll be all right after a good night's sleep."

The policemen then asked, "Will you be afraid to stay in the house with him?"

"If you can help him back to the bedroom," I said, "he'll pass out and sleep through the night."

Though we had many incidents of anger from him over the years, none had been so frightening. As usual, he remembered nothing the following morning. When I told him what happened, he said he was sorry. That was it. You couldn't talk to him about his drinking, his blackouts, and his inability to accept he had a problem. You couldn't talk to him, because he would shut you up and storm out of the house.

"Keep the peace," I would say with lips tightly clenched, "above all keep the peace." I had forced so much of his garbage inside me, I was on emotional overload. One evening, in another of his drunken stupors, he kicked me with such force I landed on the hard tile and almost cracked my elbow. I left home and stayed with a friend for two nights. I didn't know what else to do. I felt lost, confused, and ready to give up on the marriage. I couldn't stand looking at Gerry, the angry man, for another day. I had to get away, even though it meant leaving Cindy and James alone with him. That didn't worry me because I knew he would stay sober. During that time I stayed with a long-time friend, Jane Brownell, and we talked about Gerry and his drinking.

"Ollie, it's obvious to me he's an alcoholic and should be put in a treatment center."

"What's that?" I asked. I'd never heard of treatment centers. It was the mid-seventies, and alcoholism wasn't discussed as openly as it is today.

"It's your only hope, Ollie, because he can't do it alone. I know because I was there. I spent eight weeks in treatment and it saved my life."

We talked long into the night about all this, and the next morning I called Cindy and James. "Please come home, Mommy, we need you here," they pleaded. It was so sad to hear them. "That's why I'm calling," I said, "to tell you I'll be home late this afternoon."

When I arrived home, Gerry and the children were there to greet me. I was very cold to Gerry, but threw my arms around Cindy and James. They hugged me and wouldn't let go. I had no idea they thought I was never coming back.

"Why did you leave, Mom? Where did you go? We thought you were never coming home. We were so scared." Their words sounded as though I'd been gone a year.

After dinner, when Gerry and I were alone, I told him it was about time we had a long talk. I brought up his drinking and going into a treatment center, and for the first time he listened.

"I've given this a lot of thought, Ollie. I've been so worried these past two days, afraid you had left me for good, I'm determined to stop drinking altogether." He sounded so positive. "But," he added, "I'm going to do it on my own. I don't need any treatment centers, only you believing in me."

I didn't know what to say, but my inner voice warned me not to expect miracles. Gerry stopped drinking that same evening, and every day and night I held my breath. As the months went by, he became another person. He was fun again, loving and kind. The anger slipped away. There was no more screaming, blaming, or criticizing. I couldn't believe the transformation! Over and over again I would tell him how happy I was. We were all happy.

It lasted exactly six months. The first time I saw him openly pour a drink for himself, I was devastated. How could he! Wasn't the worst over? I stood there in the kitchen frozen with fear.

"When did you start drinking again?" I asked slowly.

"Now, don't get started on me, Ollie," he replied. "I'm only having one drink."

I didn't know much about alcoholism at the time, but I did know that one drink was never enough. It only took a week for him to be right back in full swing. His favorite expressions, "What else is there?" and "What's wrong with a few drinks?" were supposed to justify his actions. But not for me. I was heartbroken. The bottle once again had become his best friend, and his old familiar, belligerent, angry, alcoholic personality returned.

It was at this time that Gerry lost his job as manager of Saks Fifth Avenue, eventually joining I Magnin. I traveled to Milan twice to help develop the Marina Ferrari Collection. More and more I thought about opening our own store, and after the second trip I told Gerry I was going to look for a location in Scottsdale. Driving around by myself, I stopped at several available places only to conclude they were too small. We needed at least three-thousand square feet to do the kind of volume we anticipated. I continued the search in downtown Scottsdale and, on a whim, walked into Jordan's shop right across the street from the Sugar Bowl on Scottsdale Road. The couple who owned the store worked together. She designed a line of dramatic, hand-painted gowns, which they sold there, and he handled the business side. They also sold at wholesale to other stores outside the area during market weeks in Los Angeles and New York.

I asked him bluntly, "How do you like the retail business?"

"It's okay," he replied hesitantly, "but we're doing so well at wholesale we think we'll concentrate on that once our lease here is up."

I couldn't believe what I was hearing. "How much longer is your lease?" I boldly asked.

He didn't seem to mind and replied, "About a year and a half. Why do you ask? Are you interested in the space?"

"I might be." I tried not to let my mounting excitement give me away.

He then suggested we go to his office to discuss it further. For the next half hour, he gave me all the details regarding rent, square footage, additional adjoining space available, etc. He was willing to sublet the lease and gave me the landlord's number. I called Gerry to ask when he would like to see the space, and since both owners were there, he suggested coming right over. While I waited for him, the amazing coincidence of this possibly ending up as our store went round and round in my head. By the time Gerry arrived I was very excited. He had never been inside either and was amazed at how much bigger it was than it appeared on the outside. He saw the potential immediately. We contacted the landlord and discussed adding on the adjoining building, which he also owned. We arrived at a preliminary agreement. That was the beginning of our new store.

One month later, we took over the lease and began plans to renovate. Gerry notified I Magnin he was leaving but would stay for three weeks, enough time to find a replacement. We spent every spare minute working on floor plans, ripping out walls, ordering fixtures, and evolving our own concept for the space. The first big improvement was a new corner window, roomy enough for several mannequins. It was to become our fashion message to the public, right on Scottsdale Road with plenty of visibility. I was responsible for planning areas and merchandising them in categories, so ordering fixtures to hold them was a priority. We had custom-made fixtures that were capable of being changed around as needed. They were very new in the market and covered in camel ultrasuede, a complete departure from department store racks and rounds made of metal. They were moveable, so no area stayed the same forever. Most stores had "bins" indented in the walls with a single pipe holding the garments. Not us. Our fixtures slid into slots on flat walls and could be adjusted by height. A space-planning expert from the Los Angeles fixture company flew to Scottsdale, and together we estimated quantities for the entire store. The order would take eight to ten weeks to complete. We planned fitting rooms in various locations and put in skylights for natural light. Slowly it all came together.

Now we needed a name for the store. It turned out to be a bigger project than any of us thought. "Something that sounds European," we agreed. "Not our own name." "A three or four letter word." "Simple, with meaning." Gerry, our art expert, came up with the name, CAPRICCIO, after thumbing through his art books. He loved the painting, *Primavera*, done by Botticelli in 1482. He particularly liked the young girl dressed in a delicate floral gown strewing flowers on the ground. She was elegant and refined, projecting an image of timeless beauty. Gerry called her the Capriccio figure, and the store was named after her. Not long afterwards he painted a large copy of her, which hung in our Scottsdale store for the next twenty-three years. How many times were we asked what CAPRICCIO meant! The English dictionary calls it "caprice," "a light, free, whimsical style, a whim, a prank." It can also mean, "a sudden impulsive, unmotivated turn of mind or emotion."

I like the explanation given by a young Italian man: "When you are very much in love with your mistress, you give her everything she wants. A pearl necklace? She already has two, but to please her you give her another. A beautiful new dress? She has closets full, but you want to make her happy. A new fur coat? Of course. Nothing is too much. It is for love. That is capriccio!"

Once we decided on the name, we printed up stationery, invoices, statements, order pads, and applied CAPRICCIO to the front awning. While this was happening I organized my first buying trip to New York. Money was tight, so I flew the "red eye" to New York, leaving Phoenix about midnight and arriving at dawn. The sun was beginning to rise as we landed, and by the time I reached my hotel and unpacked I was ready for breakfast and a day of work. I had made appointments for most of the first day with vendors I had known from my buying days at Saks. It was interesting to catch up on what was happening in fashion, but it took only a few stops to discover I wasn't connecting with their collections. Our store needed a new, fresh approach that would give customers a reason to shop with us. I decided to explore the sportswear market and simply walked into showrooms and introduced myself. Everyone was interested and helped by suggesting other collections as well. By the end of the week, I had purchased enough to open our store. I had concentrated on new, young, up-and-coming designers and didn't realize at the time that youth was to become our approach, particularly in sportswear.

We found, among other surprises, a new collection of designer jeans. It was 1976, and until then the only jeans available were made by Levi Strauss. This was the first time I'd seen a collection of jeans with a fashion statement and designer logo. They were tight and skinny-legged, intended just for perfect bodies. The only way to pull them up was by lying on the fitting room floor and wriggling and squirming until they were on. (Calvin Klein jeans were first introduced with Brooke Shield's provocative pose: "Nothing gets between me and my Calvins." That advertising campaign was incredibly successful.) Designer jeans soon became an enormous business, and we constantly needed unusual tops to sell with them. We wanted to upscale the look, so we decided to pair them with beautiful silk blouses made in Italy by Pancaldi. In contrast, we also bought whimsical, collaged, cotton blouses with wrap-waisted, attached sashes designed by a young Dutch designer, Koos von den Akker. His mix of prints suggested thrift shop couture and were totally irresistible. Selling silk blouses and designer wrap tops with jeans was totally new. Up until then jeans were Levis worn with tee shirts down on the ranch.

Just a few from a selection of unusual, hand-made European belts

Next we searched for unusual belts to wear with jeans, not just brass-buckled classics but one-of-a-kind, hand-made belts with buckles that looked like modern jewelry. Cesar of Gstaad introduced us to that look. His belts were works of art. We found an assortment of designers who were unknown, located off Seventh Avenue, who gave us exclusives. We became known for our incredible belts, casually strewn on long antique tables like an invitation to a feast. Some of our most unusual belts were designed by Lisandro Sarasola who, with his native Argentinian talent, created masterpieces by gluing together bits and pieces of leather, feathers, and studs.

It was important from the beginning to plan a total look, tops to go with bottoms, belts to pull it altogether, and plenty of choices. On that first buying trip to New York, I realized that this concept would be the secret of our success. Quality and fit were important, particularly in our selection of a pants collection. Not just any pants, but beautifully cut, perfectly fitting pants in an assortment of fabrics. We looked around the market, asked questions, and finally decided on Italian pants from Zanella and French pants from le Painty. It was time-consuming to buy their lines because, after selecting a few styles, we were given endless fabric possibilities. We were very successful with these two lines and carried them from opening day until we closed our store twenty-three years later.

We had planned an "evening area" in our new store, but I didn't want the typical cocktail dress or bouffant ball gown image. We found Zoran, a young beginning designer, and saw his collection of simple silk separates at his loft in the Village. They were beautifully non-constructed pieces that flowed over the body, giving a new, soft feel. The samples were all in black, and every piece worked with every other piece. It wasn't long before he was discovered by *Vogue* and *Bazaar* as well as some top New York stores. At the same time we stumbled on Michael Katz, a young talented artist, who was just beginning the art of painting on silk. His studio was also in the Village, and we saw him at the end of the day. It was quite a first experience because his building was in a scary part of downtown. We rode up a rickety elevator, praying it would creak us up safely. When we arrived, the elevator door led right into his huge studio. At one end were his living quarters, hidden partially by sheets that were placed on a rope. His showroom consisted of a couch and two chairs with a table in the middle. The rest of the space was taken by two long tables with silk fabric stretched on them in the process of being painted. Best of all was Michael, a warm, friendly, gracious artist who greeted me like royalty. We sat down at the little table laden with white wine, cheese and crackers, and fresh fruit, and talked about his collection. He first started painting fabric for kimonos, because they were one size and fit wasn't a problem. As he showed me each piece, I jumped up and started to try them on. I asked if he could vary the styling into different lengths. "That's easy," he said, so we spent hours that afternoon planning my buy. His paintings were vivid and wild, and looked best with black backgrounds. I planned to show them over Zoran's black evening separates. The following season, for summer, we planned a group with white backgrounds and pastel paintings. We carried his collection for years and did frequent trunk shows with Michael in person.

By the time my buying trip was finished, I had seen over fifty vendors. I bought from most of them and was assured everything would be delivered before our store opened. It was very exciting to return to Phoenix and see progress on the building. We worked from early morning till late evening for the next three months. Gerry insisted on sleeping in the store for the last few weeks, even though we had already installed an alarm system. He worked with a passion, and it was obvious he loved it. The entire family was involved including Cindy (now fifteen years old) and James (nine years old). They helped with many of the smaller jobs like opening boxes and hanging up merchandise as it arrived. Gerry's daughter, Nancy, left her job as a cocktail waitress and joined us in those early days before the store opened. Her husband, Hilal, also helped, but he continued with his job as a necktie salesman until after we opened. Gerry believed in hiring the "family" because "they could be trusted." Over and over he would say, "Ollie, I want you to take Nancy and train her." She started in the receiving room after we opened, and soon afterwards was promoted to sales. In the beginning, I carried some "I-can't-shake-them" resentments towards her. I would have preferred someone with more experience, but Gerry wouldn't hear of it. "She's my *daughter*, and I'd like you to teach her the business," he insisted. In time Nancy and I warmed up to one another. I recognized her artistic talents as she created beautiful displays around the store. We put her in charge of display early on. She was developing her own clientele and soon became one of our top salespersons, along with Barbara Hagerty. I met Barbara at the hairdressers. We were sitting next to each other waiting to be called and started a conversation.

"I know your store," she said enthusiastically, "I'd love to work there."

"Are you serious?" I replied, "because if you are, come by the store later and we'll talk."

"Really? Really?" Barbara was elated. I loved her enthusiasm and openness and already knew I was going to hire her. She turned out to be the backbone of our sales staff.

TWELVE

CAPRICCIO

My Alter Ego

We opened CAPRICCIO in Scottsdale, Arizona, November of 1976. It was very exciting for Gerry and me, because it was OUR store. Instead of a party, we served white wine all day. Many of our friends came, bought clothing, and wished us well. There was a warm, tingly atmosphere those first days. We played romantic, Italian music, the latest from Milan, that really helped set the mood. Even our shopping bags were made in Milan, slick, shiny brown paper with our logo. We ordered them in several sizes and huge quantities. I'll never forget the day they arrived, looking like a ten-year supply of shopping bags! Much to our surprise, we needed to reorder after the second year. We had custom-made hangers with our logo imprinted on them, and plastic garment bags with CA-PRICCIO, CAPRICCIO, CAPRICCIO printed all over them. These little touches made our store special and appealing.

We never imagined I would need to buy more merchandise so soon. Business was phenomenal, and two months later I was on my way to New York again. After calling key vendors and pleading with them to help us out, I was able to get reorders from larger store's shipments immediately. Since we needed merchandise NOW, they were "stealing" from other orders that were ready to be shipped to them. I never forgot those people who helped us when we needed it most. I spent three days pulling immediate delivery from them and flew back to Phoenix thrilled with the results. When I returned home, Gerry was full of news.

"Ollie, you can't imagine how busy the store has been. There are customers I've never met who are buying thousands of dollars at a time. You'll have to go to the California market in a few days to pick up some more merchandise." It was unbelievable!

Oscar de la Renta made regular trips to present his complete collection in formal fashion shows

One of the best decisions we made early on was not to have charge accounts. It was the mid-seventies and the beginning of credit cards. We welcomed Master Charge, Visa, and American Express. That meant no bookkeeping for us, and we received our money from the bank the next day. Many of our customers were used to saying, "Charge it to my account." It took time to re-educate them to charge it to their credit cards. Often Gerry or I would personally explain to them why we wouldn't open personal accounts. It was very simple. We wanted to be paid immediately, and charge accounts could take months to pay.

Bill Blass visited Saks Fifth Avenue to present his collection. We became good friends.

The day-to-day routine was never boring. Gerry was back to his old self again, and I found myself looking at him with pride. He had slimmed down and was once again wearing his custom

Hugh Downs, Glendon Swarthout and guests at our home in Phoenix.

made-in-Milan suits using Oleg Cassini's tailor. Gerry was about 5′9″, and I secretly wished he were taller. He had a full head of dark hair that was beginning to grey at the temples. He was handsome in an Irish open-faced way, with a prominent nose and a chin that doubled with time. His blue-grey eyes crinkled whenever he laughed, and in those early years there was plenty of light-heartedness. He enjoyed his own jokes most of all. He was very open on the surface, but it was impossible to reach him underneath. He had secrets that followed him to his grave. He would disappear in the afternoons and not return until five o'clock. Some days he stayed at home and painted. I was surprised one evening when I returned home from work to find the subject of a painting sitting on his easel was a young, blonde girl. She looked about twenty-five. When I asked him who she was, he angrily replied, "You don't know her." His tone of voice said, "It's none of your business." At any moment he could shift into one of his unexplainable mood swings, and I never knew what would set him off.

I remember one occasion when we were at a dinner party about

Robert Goulet stealing a kiss on the cheek. I didn't mind at all.

Oleg Cassini and Gerry McNamara were good friends for years.

Pauline Trigere (in dark glasses) making a personal appearance to presented her fashion show.

to be seated, when Gerry came over to me, took me by the arm, and announced, "Ollie, let's get out of here. I can't stand these people for another minute." There was nothing restrained about him. I was humiliated. He didn't care that it was the last time we were invited there. His erratic behavior became worse with time.

Gerry always had a tendency to put on weight quickly. When he did, it all landed in his stomach and chin. His suits were tailored to be tight, and a few of the so-called men around town made fun of his European clothes. They only wore Brooks Brothers or J. Press with button-down shirts, and I found their appearances boring compared to Gerry's. His shirts were custom tailored, plastered to his body, in shocking pink, purple, or vivid blue. His ties were striking. The total package was uniquely him. What really made Gerry, though, went way beyond the way he dressed. He had an infectious personality and took over a room when he entered. He had everyone laughing within minutes. At a dinner table he would mesmerize those around him with his knowledge of art. He would talk about Vermeer and the limited number of paintings he had made or about the early works of any artist and how they changed with time. He charmed the women with his easy ways and slightly wicked personality. At his best, no one could match him. At his worst, he turned into another person.

In the store, he would play his role of proprietor with ease and pride. He took over the financial and business ends of things while I did the buying and promotional parts. He was perfectly happy with the arrangement, as was I. Business continued to explode, and within a year we knew we had outgrown the "little" store. Customers loved us. The press promoted us. The market buzzed about this new boutique in Scottsdale, Arizona. I was caught up with buying, analyzing, controlling inventories, and not getting carried away with our success. Gerry was busy on the selling floor, greeting customers, and in the office, adding up our daily sales to deposit each morning. He had hired his son-in-law, Hilal Chaboun, early on to assist. He taught Hilal about the retail business, and not too long after Hilal took over many of Gerry's responsibilities.

Much to our surprise, after being in business for only one year, we received a call from Ben Kelts, a wealthy businessman in La Jolla. He knew us by reputation and wondered if we were interested in a second location for CAPRICCIO. We listened.

"My wife has a boutique on Prospect Street called BEVERLY WEST. We're divorcing and aren't quite sure the best way to end our business operations. The store is only a year old, beautifully decorated, and ready for a new tenant immediately."

"How much inventory do you have?" we asked.

"Too much," he replied, "but if you can get rid of it by conducting sales until it's all gone, I'll give you the store at no cost."

We couldn't believe it. We had no intention of a second store after only one year in business, but this sounded too good. The next day we flew over to La Jolla to meet the owner and see the boutique. We were impressed with the store's beauty.

"My wife had good taste, and she hired one of the best decorators from Beverly Hills to pull it all together," Ben remarked then added, "I'm going to leave you to look around by yourselves. Call me when you're finished and we'll talk."

Gerry was getting anxious and couldn't wait to see the rest of the building. The store was hardly built to do "big" business, and it looked like a society wife's version of the perfect backdrop for displays. There was a huge espresso machine on one wall and very little hanging space. Most of the inventory was sweaters, and they were everywhere. A contemporary round glass table in the front center as you walked in was filled with piles-by-color sweaters. There were wicker chairs for seating. In the back area were several tiny fitting rooms and a room to receive merchandise. We were surprised to find an upper level that turned out to be crammed with boxes and boxes of prior season purchases.

"My God," I remarked, "this looks like a two year's supply of inventory!"

We kept looking, and every time we opened a closet door there was more merchandise piled on shelves and on the floor. Half of it was still in original boxes that had never been opened. All of it was saleable and attractive, but was prior season and dated. We took a complete count and were staggered by the quantity and dollar value, but it would be up to us to mark it all down and promote a sale.

We met with Ben that afternoon outlining our plan. Everything would be marked down to half and the sale would be advertised as a "change of ownership." The customers swarmed in, and a week later half the merchandise was sold. We then went on radio and television announcing, "Everything is now at seventy-five per cent off." This attracted enough people to sell out most of the balance. Ben removed all that was left, and we took over the building once the lease was negotiated with the owner.

Once again we were back renovating another store. It was really a little jewel, and I said to Gerry, "What a great idea. When business is slow in Scottsdale (June, July, August), it's peak season in La Jolla, and when it's slow in La Jolla (January, February, March) it's busiest in Scottsdale."

It also turned out to be a huge success, and we were constantly transferring merchandise back and forth from Scottsdale to La Jolla. We realized early on the need for a bigger store, but it wasn't until four years later that we had the opportunity to buy a magnificent two story building at 6919 La Jolla Boulevard. It was thought by many to be a foolish move because it was not on Girard or Prospect Street. Against all odds, we renovated the building and made it into another successful shop. In addition, the second floor was magically turned into a beautiful private apartment for our family.

During these same four years, CAPRICCIO, SCOTTSDALE, established its reputation as the best, most exciting, new boutique in town. We carried unusual styles and concentrated on designers not carried by the bigger stores. In 1976 the only competition we had was another boutique, MICHELE. She had her own clientele, who were very loyal. The two big stores, SAKS FIFTH AVENUE and I MAGNIN, were the first to bring high fashion to Arizona. Previously referred to as "Cow-Country," Phoenix was growing rapidly with a new sophistication and attitude. You could feel it happening. It wasn't long before we were asked to put on luncheon fashion shows to raise funds for local charities. The average attendance was usually five hundred women, and as Gerry always said, "It's the best advertising we can do."

Those years in the "little store" were very happy. Gerry and I did a lot of socializing, attending most of the big Balls, going to parties, entertaining at home, and keeping busy. It was important that we be "visible" in the community. From 1976–1980, the store built its reputation. We were amazed at our profitable dollar-per-square-foot volume and our high turnover: eight to ten turns a year. Our markdowns were very low for a "high end" boutique: averaging eight to ten per cent. As we analyzed all this, it was obvious we had outgrown the space and needed a bigger store. We had started a shoe department called "Shoe Biz" and wanted to add a fine jewelry department, and furs, but we simply had no room. Sportswear was our most important category, and we expanded that department when I went to Europe for my first buy.

I spent half of my trip in Milan, where the most fashion excitement was happening, and Florence, where I found smaller vendors who produced primarily for the Italians. It was 1980-81 and big designers like Versace and Armani were about to enter the fashion scene. I bought from established manufacturers known for their unusual sweaters, blouses, and leathers rather than collections as a whole. There were beautiful pants, skirts, and jackets to work with them. In the Fall we might buy tweed bottoms to go with tweedsy sweaters or camel bottoms with cream or camel tops. In Spring-Summer we would plan a total pink story and find pink silk or gabardine skirts and pants with matching silk blouses, tee shirts, nubby sweaters, and jackets. These coordinated groups flew out of the store, and we could never get enough. Reorders from Europe were impossible, so we placed larger quantities on our initial buy. Some of my favorite vendors from Italy at that time were Pancaldi, who made beautiful silk blouses; Umberto Ginochietti, a genius at tweedsy sweaters and coordinating bottoms; Roberto Cavalli, early on known for his unique leathers and suedes; and Cavalli's sister, Lieta, who had a cottage industry of ladies who transformed yarn into gossamer sweaters and cobwebby creations.

I loved going to their showrooms in those early days. Roberto Cavalli showed his collection in his factory in Florence, where the pungent smell of leather permeated the air. I was seated at a small table as they wheeled a rack of leather jackets and pants next to me. Hardly anyone spoke English, so I selected what I liked amidst the activity of rustling patterns and workers rushing back and forth. I wrote my orders sitting in a corner set up in the factory. Roberto darted in and out with a big smile and his usual laid-back demeanor. I gulped with each purchase, because they were very expensive but totally irresistible.

"The heck with it." I said to myself. "If I find them so tempting, so will the customers." I was right. From those beginning days forward, my buy increased with each trip.

One year Roberto and his wife threw a big party at their home during market week. Buyers and friends from many countries were there speaking a variety of languages, but almost everyone also spoke English. Roberto's house was on a hill in Florence filled with vineyards that produced grapes for delicious Cavalli wine. He also had a helicopter and pad on top of the hill that was used for skiing trips to Switzerland. The house was completely filled with candle-light when he entertained, giving a soft, romantic glow throughout. There were about fifty guests, and we all talked about fashion as we ate home-made pasta and salad. Roberto's beautiful wife was a former Miss Austria whom he met while judging a Miss Universe contest. She helped design and work on all his collections.

Buying in Europe was completely different from buying in New York. The important collections would always present formal fashion shows with three parts: before, during, and after. Before each show, hundreds of buyers would collect outside the doors where the show was to be held. We clutched our entry tickets for fear of losing them, and when the doors opened we rushed, like beetles descending on Kansas, in search of our reserved seats. Since we all came early, there was always plenty of time to people-watch. Everybody seemed to know somebody, so there was plenty of hand-waving, big smiles, and ha-ha-I-got-a-better-seat-than-you-did. The front row seats were always filled with major store buyers, merchandise managers, and store presidents. These people often would stand up filled with self-importance and, with backs to runway, search the audience for deserved recognition.

"Hello, there, Bill. How are things in Chicago?" "Business is fair." " Have you seen Dolce's line?" "You look great!" "Have you done something to your face, come onnnnnn?" It was their moment. They were Kings for the Day.

All the important shows were totally jammed with each seat reserved, and it didn't take long for seats to fill up until there was standing room only. It was exciting to be part of all this drama when houselights went off, show music blasted out, and all eyes were glued to the runway. Anticipation was intense as model after model emerged and in perfect syncopation strutted down the runway after presenting a tableau on stage of the "first group." As many as fifty models were sometimes used in these expensive fashion shows intended mainly for the press. Their cameramen crouched around the runways, clicking away for pictures that would appear the next day in newspapers around the world. When the show was finished, all the models reappeared on stage to give homage to the designer walking alone down the runway. The applause was deafening as the music played louder and louder until the last model walked off stage. Buyers would then rush off to their next shows, euphoric from the effects of this one, comparing notes with one another, and preparing for a repeat mob-scene.

The European shows were always held in March for Fall Collections and in October for Spring Collections. My schedule of shows and writing appointments filled my entire day, each day, up to ten o'clock if necessary when I was writing orders in the showrooms. I spent most of my time in Milan, but I also went to Paris for certain collections, and to London. It was hard work, and endless hours were spent trying to place the orders correctly. I was always sure of quality from the Italians, whether it was their fabrics, shoes, knitwear, or leathers. Combined with the creativity of designers like Giorgio Armani, Gianni Versace, Emanuel Ungaro, and many others, the "Made in Italy" label was always an important selling point.

Giorgio Armani was my favorite designer, and over the years most of my personal wardrobe came from his collections. He also received the biggest CAPRICCIO orders. He started out as a menswear designer, and his first women's collection consisted of jackets made from menswear fabrics. He soon added pants and skirts, then blouses and sweaters, all in coordinating colors but in different fabrics. It was easy to recognize a woman in an Armani, because Giorgio had his own particular "look." One year during "market week" in Milan, Giorgio threw a big party in his beautiful palazzo, inviting about two hundred guests. There was a huge buffet, music, and dancing, and although Giorgio was very shy he played the host and mingled with all of us. He always had a deep tan, and his beautiful, piercing blue eyes looked directly into yours as he spoke. Every season he would entertain the buyers, but often I wasn't in Milan at the same time.

When I returned from one of my European trips in 1980, Gerry met me at the airport with some unexpected news. I had so much to tell him, but I was more anxious to hear what he had to say first. "What's up?" I asked. "Something good, I hope."

"Ollie, we've been approached by some Canadian developers who want to meet with us tomorrow to talk about a new retail complex they are planning in Scottsdale."

"I think it's about time we looked for something bigger," I added, "and maybe this is the answer."

By the time we reached home, the pluses and minuses of moving were discussed and the pluses won. Now, all we needed to know was where, how big, and how much.

The next day, as we walked into the offices of Lingal Equities, we were greeted by Dewey Beucler, who introduced us to John Hamilton and partners. About a year before we had been approached by Dewey regarding a shopping center plan that looked like every other shopping center plan around. A drive-in mall with clusters of little shops hardly excited us enough to leave our charming little store. Gerry suggested they go back to the drawing boards, visit places of timeless beauty, like Florence, Italy, and get inspired to create something unique for Scottsdale. They listened to Gerry and did exactly that. They sent architects and planners to Italy to find that magical place, and after looking for weeks, finally decided on an ancient walled village northeast of Florence called St. Gimignano. When we walked into the offices of Lingal Equities that sunny day, we had no idea what to expect. Imagine our surprise to see, for the first time, a miniature model of the Borgata of Scottsdale inspired by the real thing back in Italy. Complete with seven towers, courtyards with undulating stone that looked like monks had trodden on them for centuries, a bubbling fountain, and about forty stores and restaurants, the Borgata was about to become a reality. John Hamilton gave us the whole pitch, and by the time he finished I knew this was it for both of us. We left with an appointment the following day to discuss details.

On our way back to the store, we talked about this new adventure. How much space would we want, where in the center to locate, what kind of rent to pay? We decided Gerry should negotiate the deal alone. We had been told we were the first tenants Lingal Equities wanted to sign up, so we had our choice of location and size. In addition, Gerry wanted to work with the architects to plan the interior and exterior to accommodate purchases of antique architectural doors, windows, etc. When it was all arranged, we had a sweetheart lease and a 10,000-square-ft. store in an ideal location.

It took almost a year to complete our building. We went to Europe and to auctions to find interesting antiques for the store. While in Florence, Gerry insisted we return to a shop where he had fallen in love with a marble fountain twenty years ago.

"Who knows, it might still be there, and if it is, we're going to buy it," he announced.

"Gerry, you're crazy. It can't possibly still be there after all this time," I muttered.

He wanted to buy it twenty years before but never had a room high enough to place it. As we arrived at the store and looked in the window, there in the exact same corner was this beautiful, white, Carrara marble fountain. We could hardly believe it, after twenty years! It was spectacular, with swans and dolphins dribbling water into two bowls, and at the top a bronze "boy with dolphin" also dribbling water. The original sculpture of the boy was created by Verrochio in 1470 and sits in the Palazzo Vecchio in Florence, Italy. The entire fountain, with the boy, measured over ten feet high, perfect for the soaring entryway of our new store. It was the focal point when you came in, and with the gentle, welcoming drip, drip, drip, it made a lasting impression on all who entered. At Christmas time, we would place lush garlands of pine crowded with Della Robbia-like fruit from the top of the fountain curving around and down to its base. We would wind miniature bee lights all over the garlands and aim a spotlight on it all. Masses of red poinsettias were placed inside and outside the base of the fountain, and long, floral garlands were attached to four sparkling chandeliers above it.

In addition to the fountain, we found other treasures in England, like the Lloyds of London massive, ebony wood entry doors we used for our main entrance. They were surrounded by windows with bronze inserts, which gave the doors a majestic look. Above the doors, we installed one huge window to add more daylight. We added a smaller version of double doors for our side entrance.

Continuing on our search, we found a mid-eighteenth century pine-paneled room complete with fireplace, corner cabinet, and doors. It had been the walls of an English barrister's office. "We'll use this in the sportswear department," exclaimed Gerry. "It'll be perfect!" And it was. After installing the paneling a few months later, we placed pine beams on the ceiling and leather-colored, twelve-inch tile on the floor. We even planned two separate fitting rooms with pine-paneled walls for this area.

One of our surprise finds was a self-contained, antique English pub. "Let's use it as a wrap desk where we write up sales," I thought. It turned out to be a perfect solution, and for twenty years customers gathered around it to finalize their buys.

When we found a pair of massive, decorative iron gates, we wondered what to do with them. Gerry came up with the idea of using them as "room dividers" between the upper and lower levels of the sportswear area and the main floor. It took six men to lift them into place, but once up they were incredibly beautiful.

Of all our finds, my favorite were the antique, leaded, conservatory windows from Staffordshire, England. They were used in our designer salon as a complete wall from floor to ceiling, allowing sunlight to twinkle through the colored panels all day. It was a peaceful place, even on a hectic day.

All these important architectural antiques gave CAPRICCIO its unique ambience, but now we needed some large pieces of furniture. We found them finally in an antique store in La Jolla called A La Douce France. The owners, Arthur and Josianne Hanks, had an incredible selection of armoires, large tables, desks, buffets, etc. Josianne was French whose family were third-generation antiquaires in Paris with a shop in the old antique district on the Rue de St.Pere. All the furniture in their La Jolla store came from her parents, who had entrée to the best antiques throughout France. We purchased a number of items from them to put in our Borgata store as well as our home. Imagine our surprise when we were told a few months later that Arthur and Josianne were getting a divorce and she was returning to Paris. All the antiques were on sale, and when Arthur told us the building was also going to be sold, we immediately expressed an interest in buying it. This was in 1982, one year after we had opened the Borgata store.

We opened CAPRICCIO at the Borgata November 2, 1981. I had been calling vendors for weeks to remind them to ship our orders by the end of October. They were wonderful about it, and since we needed to vacate the little store as well as move into the Borgata, it was pretty hectic. All our fixtures from the little store were able to be used, and additional ones arrived on time ready to be filled with merchandise. The finished store was beautiful, with flowers everywhere and displays throughout telling our fashion message. Borgata management planned a huge party in the central courtyard the evening we opened. By then most of the center was complete, and this "by invitation only" event was our official introduction to the community. Tables were laden with food and desserts placed amongst spectacular floral arrangements, with live music setting the mood. All forty of us from CAPRICCIO were there to show guests around the store. With the huge entry doors wide open and the fountain sprinkling hellos, it was very inviting. Clients were amazed and wanted to see it all. We now had a fine jewelry department as you entered and a shoe area on the opposite side. When told we had twelve fitting rooms, each completely different, customers wanted to see them all. They were not your typical department store cubicles, but spacious rooms with colorful walls, paintings, and skylights for natural light. Customers pulled merchandise to be held until the next day for them to try.

"Barbara, make sure you hold these. I'll be in tomorrow." "Hide these in the back. I'll see you tomorrow." "Don't lose these. I'll see you tomorrow." Happy, profitable reactions for us!

The entire project of the store had put Gerry deliriously immersed in creativity. He was always happiest doing something artistic, and this was the single biggest project he had ever attempted. Now that it was complete, memories remained of "I can't wait to see the pine paneling installed in sportswear," or, "The fountain is going to take a lot of muscle to install," "I'm going to remove every single bronze doohickey from the door's adjoining windows and polish them for the first time in fifty years." (Lloyds of London had demolished their building in London and built a new one, and we were the lucky buyers of their former main entrance doors.) We did nothing but talk about the store for eight months, and now that it was completed we were ready to get down to business. Long hours and hard work—incredible business beckoned.

CAPRICCIO had been open only a few months when we heard about Arthur and Josianne Hanks' pending divorce and the sale of their building at 6919 La Jolla Boulevard and all the antiques.

"This sounds like a perfect solution for more space in La Jolla," Gerry and I agreed. "It all depends on the price."

The building was relatively new, having been built by the Hanks only a few years before. We decided to fly to San Diego the next day to finalize a bid. After negotiating back and forth for several weeks, we finally arrived at a price we both agreed to, and the building was ours. But it didn't end there. The apartment above the store was also filled with beautiful antiques, and since we planned to use it as our home when visiting the La Jolla store, we were interested in

Opening the new Capriccio store in La Jolla. We decided to purchase the building and transform the first floor into a business and the second floor into a private home.

buying many of the pieces. They were selling everything, because shipping back to France would be very expensive. We purchased a 17th-century oak dining room table, thirteen feet long, that came from a monastery, as well as eight dining chairs to go with it, two buffets on separate walls, and three 18th-century brass chandeliers. In the kitchen, we bought their 17th-century cherry wood table with six oak dining chairs, and a tall, 16th-century "meuble deux corps" (double kitchen cabinet) in walnut. Since we were going to live there, we left everything we purchased right where they were. Many more pieces were shipped to the Borgata store, including a "bibliotheque de boiserie," (walnut bookcase) from the mid-1800s that was almost ten-feet high and eight-feet wide. We placed it in the shoe department as you entered the store on a huge wall that needed an important piece. It was a perfect backdrop for shoe display.

We did more alterations to the La Jolla building before we could move in, including a large addition in the back. Many structural features needed reinforcing, and the entire building was painted after corner quoins were added. Formerly, the back of the building had been used as a "warehouse" for receiving containers from France; it needed new flooring and entry doors. We made fitting rooms with twelve-foot-high pairs of 18th-century doors. We used similar doors in the apartment above, which gave a European feeling to it. The upstairs was on two levels, and the entire upper level was transformed with 17th-century parquet floors, which we purchased from the Hanks. When we first saw the flooring, it was a huge pile of dusty pieces of wood that needed a keen eye to appreciate their intrinsic beauty. After sorting the pieces by appropriate design and laying them down in various rooms, we saw the floors come back to life. Waxing and polishing transformed them. Several places even had centuries old, built-in squeaks, as though the wood was sighing in gratitude for its new home.

After the small store on Prospect Street, the CAPRICCIO building at 6919 La Jolla Boulevard appeared immense. We decided to celebrate the opening of the new store with a huge party, inviting more than two hundred people. We hired a small band, had a dance floor, and set up round tables and chairs throughout the store as well as under the tents outside. The French Gourmet catered the party. Then it began to rain, and all the tables and chairs outside were crowded into the store. It made everyone relax and have fun. The apartment above was open so guests could wander freely up and down. "Queen Elizabeth" made an appearance, dressed all in white. She was an actress from Hollywood, who caused a sensation walking slowly through the crowd saying, "Helloooo, hellooo, what a fine pahty." "You look absolutely divine." "My Deah, I'm so glad you could come." Her head would sway from side to side and her feather headpiece would ripple. The Press loved it. All the funds raised that evening went to UCSD Medical Center. We helped many future "worthy causes" by putting on fashion shows in La Jolla and Scottsdale. It was one way to give back to the community.

Customers over the years loved personal tours of the stores, and they were always interested in knowing more about the many unusual antiques. When I graduated from Cornell and moved to New York City, I began a love affair with beautiful antiques. Even when earning only twenty-eight dollars a week in the early fifties, I would save enough to buy a piece here and there. My first purchase was a tall Mademoiselle clock from France that I found in Stuart Blaine's and Bob Booth's antique shop in New York. It was unusual because it curved into round sides, like a woman's hips, and was made entirely from exquisite fruitwood. Shopping on Third Avenue for bargains never worked for me, so I began regular visits to Macy's Little Corner Shop to search for pieces I could use. I bought my first armoire there in 1955 for $195.00. For some strange reason the interior had been fitted with custom made drawers, which turned out to be very useful. My next big purchase was a beautiful, late 17th-century French dining table with six tall back chairs , made of oak and walnut with a patina only age could induce. I bought them from my friend, Lewis Koser, when I was renovating the brownstone. He had found them in the Corner Shop at Macy's and decided they would look better in my dining room. I still have them in my home today.

There's a story behind each purchase, but the constant always remains: when I want to be good to myself, I buy an antique. Every special piece is still with me, like so many obedient children available for a loving look or caress.

I occasionally imagine their previous lives, "Don't you dare place that wine glass on me. I haven't had any rings or spots in a hundred years," said the outspoken elegant French desk.

"You can't put those hot dishes on my newly waxed surface without place mats," moaned the worried-all-the-time dining table. "They will ruin my perfect appearance."

I liked their imaginary gossip most of all. "Look at Emma; trying to woo Henry. He's scared to death of her," said the clock to the armoire. "Oh, I don't know, she's pretty persuasive. I overheard them talking and my, oh, my, there they go out in the garden together."

"That looks like a fait accompli to me," whispered the armoire smugly.

"A choo!" sneezed the exquisitely carved, marble topped entry table. "Look at me. I'm the first thing guests see when they walk in here, and I'm full of offensive dust right down to my delicate cabriolet legs!"

"I promise you'll be dusted thoroughly tomorrow when the cleaning lady comes." I tell it very gently. "But for now let me rub the surface dust off your marble top."

"Ummm, ummm, ummmmm," moaned the table, "I'm getting exci–i–ited. . . .

The stories these antiques could tell if only they talked!

THIRTEEN

Kids

It's Tough to Be a Mom

While Gerry and I were immersed in buying antiques, helping build the Borgata store, taking care of business at the little store, and renovating our newly purchased La Jolla building, Cindy and James were growing up. Cindy was fifteen now and attended Camelback High. I still remember her every morning, whizzing down the driveway on her bicycle to school. Although I loved her dearly, we weren't very close at that time. I was never there for her nor for James when they came home from school. I was a chronic workaholic, and the store became my obsession. Fortunately, Cindy was involved with church activities and spent much of her free time with Carol Probert, her best friend during those teen age years. By now she had her own horse and would go off riding by herself after school and on weekends.

When Cindy was about fourteen, I noticed a change in her. She became afraid of her room at night. She never paid particular attention to her draperies being drawn, but one night after I returned from a buying trip to New York, she closed her draperies tightly and told me she had seen strange men outside her window. She also heard noises in the hallway outside her room and imagined there were intruders. Whether they were in her dreams or not, we never knew, but that fear lingered with her until she left for college four years later.

Now eighteen, she was off to college, and in the Fall of 1980 entered Colorado State University in Fort Collins, Colorado. At first she considered majoring in veterinary medicine because of her love of horses, but eventually changed to medical technology. Cindy always made friends easily, so I didn't worry about her adjustment to college. I knew she welcomed the change because of what was going on at home.

She spent every summer with us in La Jolla during her college years, when we usually took vacation trips together. One year we planned a cruise through the Greek Islands, continuing on to Italy, France, and England. My lasting memory of the cruise portion of that trip was the morning I caught James suspended three quarters of the way through the porthole in our cabin. One more inch and he would have fallen through and into the choppy ocean. I grabbed his dangling legs, but James kicked them loose, and until he decided he was bored with that position, I left him alone. He finally wriggled back inside the ship, and much to our relief, just sat there grinning with I-did-it success.

Other times we traveled to Idaho, Wyoming, the Grand Canyon, Sedona, and other interesting places in Arizona. Both children loved to take these trips, because the whole family was together. Those were some of the good years.

James was only eight years old when Cindy was fourteen. He was difficult to manage, and if he didn't get his own way there would be an unrelenting scene. He was also very hyper, but could concentrate on things that interested him like model airplanes, engines, and astronomy. We marvelled at his intelligence, as did everyone else who met him. At home he was affectionate and happy, particularly when he received individual attention. He loved to read and, as a little boy, always asked us to read a good night story, or two, or three. Early on he was a charmer. We always had animals around, and he and Otto, our dog, were pals. James even learned to ride his father's horses, but he didn't have the same passion his sister had for them. We were amazed by his perpetual curiosity and endless questions.

At school, however, he was disruptive in classrooms, talked out of turn, made noises, and generally upset his teachers. Every semester I was called in to review his behavior. It was always the same. "James is very bright, but he doesn't perform up to his potential." Phoenix Country Day was his first school, followed by Madison 1, Brophy Prep, Camelback High, and finally La Jolla High. It was the same at each school. He had no desire to excel even though he was extremely intelligent. Grades on his report cards were barely passing. When he was a young teenager, I was not aware of his marijuana smoking, but every morning it was torturous trying to awaken him for school.

"Please," he would mumble, "let me have five more minutes of sleep."

Every single morning, it was the same. Trying to get him to eat breakfast was just as bad. He was never hungry, so I always made sure he was given food he liked: bacon and eggs or cereal for breakfast with fresh orange juice and a glass of milk. At least that way he had something in his stomach to get him through the morning. This went on until he finished high school.

For companionship, we hired a young Japanese student to be with James after school. He lived in our small guest house-cabana and was a very interesting addition to the family. When he finished his schooling at UCSD he made plans to return to Japan. He had been with us about one year and we were sad to see him leave. I took him aside the day he left and told him, "Masataka, you've been a wonderful friend to James, patient and kind, and we will all miss you."

He looked at James and with a resonant, "Sayonara," gave him a big hug, jumped on his motorcycle, and sped off into his future. We never saw or heard from him again.

Not too much later, we hired another student from UCSD. He was an easy-going, hip, Irish young man named Ed Reilly. He lived with us for several years. When James was an adult he told me it was Ed who had introduced him to marijuana. I first found out James was smoking pot when he was on his way to the Phoenix Country Club to watch a golf tournament with one of his friends. He was in his early teens. As he was leaving, I noticed a bulge in his jacket and asked him what it was.

"Oh, it's nothing, Mom. Just some stuff I need."

"Show me," I asked. His behavior had triggered my curiosity.

I had no idea why he was so secretive. Quickly I reached into his jacket and something that looked like a long pipe fell to the floor. Clunk. Clunk. James looked at it, and I stared at it.

"What in the world is that?" I asked

"Oh, it's just a bong, Mom. Don't worry about it." I had no idea what a bong was, nor what it was used for. I had never seen one before.

"What do you do with this thing?" I wanted to know.

"I just smoke a little pot with it now and then," he said with a tone in his voice of my-God,-what's-she-going-to-do-about-this now!

"You smoke WHAT!" I exclaimed. "YOU SMOKE POT? POT? DIRTY, STINKING POT?"

I was so shaken at that moment my brain went into fast-forward. I visualized James in handcuffs being taken to jail, and all he could say was, "What's wrong with smoking a little pot?"

"Empty your pockets and throw any pot you have into the toilet," I commanded, "and if there is any in your room, get rid of it NOW." I was very angry.

He had a little packet of the stuff on him and reluctantly handed it to me. "Now you can leave this bong thing and go to the golf tournament with your friend," I said. ""We'll talk about this with your father tonight." I found it hard to believe that he would dare go through police-supervised entryways at the Club with absolutely no fear of being caught with pot on him.

Unfortunately, James never thought of consequences. He just did it. When punishment was imposed, he would simply shrug his shoulders. While he was at Brophy Prep playing on the golf team, he was infuriated by a bad shot. Instead of accepting it and going on, he threw his golf club in anger and strode off. The coach had no patience with James. He threw him off the golf team and

James at 17. He's James now, not Jamie, and a junior at Brophy Prep.

wouldn't take him back. It was sad because James loved golf and was a very good player. When I asked him about it, he just said, "it wasn't fair."

Another incident occurred in the second half of his junior year when he was headed for the school bathrooms. One of the school guards followed him and peered through the glass-topped door. He saw James pull something out of the back of the toilet water tank and immediately rushed in. He asked James to give him the plastic bag. James was really startled, handed it to him, and off they went to the principal's office. It turned out to be pot which was strictly forbidden in this Catholic school run by Jesuits. James was expelled from Brophy when he only had a year and a half left till graduation. It was a big blow to him, but all he could say was, "Everybody at Brophy smokes pot!" What James did was wrong, but I still begged the head of Brophy to give him one more chance. "Only a year and a half until graduation," I pleaded. They wouldn't budge. As a result, James was enrolled in public school at Camelback High.

When this happened, I had a long talk with James regarding lying to me about smoking pot and using it in school. "Didn't you know you'd be expelled from Brophy if they caught you? Weren't you afraid of that happening?" I was heartsick and didn't feel I was reaching James at all.

"Oh, Mom, it's all right. I'll just go to Camelback High. I don't think it's right they followed me into the bathroom and caught me. Almost all the kids at Brophy smoke pot. Why did they pick on me?" James was rationalizing the whole incident.

We talked for a long time about his future, going to college, improving his grades, and most of all about living up to his potential. Ed Reilly lived with us during James' tumultuous, young teenage years. He would drop James off at school and pick him up daily. I asked him many times to encourage James not to smoke pot and to work on his studies to raise his grades. He was a potential A student receiving D's. I felt totally helpless, because the store needed me and so did James. I thought that someone closer to James' age could reach him, but little did I know Ed was smoking along with him.

James loved Brophy Prep, and was very disappointed when asked to leave. I don't think he ever imagined it could happen. When it did, and he was faced with that reality, he never said a word. He held it all inside. It was another example of his dare-devil behavior and refusal to consider the consequences of his actions. He just couldn't help it. During his teens he had two automobile accidents. One occurred when he tried to outrun the police and finally stopped abruptly, hitting a cable junction box and damaging the front end of our car. He was charged with "speed greater than reasonable and prudent" and "altered driver's license." His punishment was a two-hundred-dollar fine, probation for a year, and meetings with his probation officer regularly. James was very frightened during all this legal procedure, which required a lawyer, court appearances, and financial output. Gerry and I were very angry at James, but we were relieved that neither he nor his passengers were hurt. James was sixteen when this accident happened. It was another of his daring attempts to evade being caught. He really thought he could get away with it.

His second accident involved a car hitting him broadside while he was racing across the street in our Pontiac. He later admitted he was "sure" he could make it across the street before the car on his right reached the intersection. Fortunately, again, neither driver was hurt when the impact occurred. Our car was totaled. The other driver had little damage to the front of his car, but we were left with the expenses and replacement of our car.

We could almost have predicted trouble ahead when James, at eight years of age, crawled into our maid's car parked in the driveway. He somehow started the car while sitting in the driver's seat, and as it began to move down the sloping driveway he screamed, "Mommy, Mommy." I came running out with Maria right behind me to see the car roll down the driveway and make a sudden stop across the main street curb. Fortunately, no traffic was there to cause a more serious accident. We ran down the driveway to see if James was all right, and there he sat clearly frightened but still somewhat pleased with himself. No damage was done to the car, but it was just another example of his fearlessness.

James always had an adventuresome spirit. As a little boy, he was fascinated with astronomy, so we bought him a good telescope. He scanned the skies for years afterwards and to this day still uses that telescope. When he was two he could take apart and put back together a telephone that we had given him so he wouldn't touch ours. He had a natural gift for fixing things and was very curious about how they worked. We'd give him a project of interest and he would get completely absorbed, whether it was building Legos or model airplanes or collecting stamps. He was happiest in his own little world, and when interrupted, he would rebel unless something else of interest was offered.

Throughout those early years and into high school, James had difficulties in the classroom. I used to wonder why he wasn't motivated and finally realized he must have been bored by public school teaching with large classes. James needed one-on-one attention in a private school with small classes, something we couldn't afford at the time. If only he had been singled out by one teacher who recognized his potential and encouraged him along the way, it might have changed his life.

At home he and his father would either have pleasant times together with some of James' hobbies or screaming episodes that often ended up with slamming doors or leaving the house. On one occasion James and Gerry were eye-to-eye almost touching each other's foreheads in the midst of a huge battle. Gerry threatened to "beat the Hell out of James" while James, full of anger, exploded.

"Go ahead, Dad, hit me. Hit me!" I came running in, knowing Gerry was drunk and anything could happen. "Hit me," James repeated. " I dare you. I'm as big as you now and you don't scare me anymore!"

I tried to separate them, and in the scuffle Gerry almost fell. He stumbled out of the room swearing and yelling, collapsed on the couch, and immediately passed out. For months our evenings were the same. Gerry started drinking at noon with lunch, and would continue late afternoon into dinner time. By the time we finished our meal, he would get up from the table and stagger back to the family room. I would find him passed out on the couch. Night after night. Month after month. Year after year.

Gerry refused to accept the reality that he was drinking too much, and I refused to accept the reality that I could do nothing to stop him. He became more and more difficult to live with and anything could set him off—a look, an innocent comment, or any reference to his drinking. It was difficult to have a conversation with him for fear of saying the wrong thing, and I found myself constantly "on guard" verbally.

What happened over the years? Our marriage was falling apart and I didn't know how to recapture those happy early times. The bottle had taken away Gerry's humor and zest for life, and he was turning into an angry, negative person. I was beginning to worry that James and Gerry would have a huge fight ending up with someone hurt. Their fights were more frequent and much more intense. There were days when Gerry and I hardly spoke to each other, making the situation even more difficult. He was depressed and withdrawn, and I could do nothing to help. All he did was read, drink, and complain. In the summer of 1985 I went to La Jolla with James, as usual, and Gerry stayed in Phoenix. Normally he would visit regularly, but that summer he didn't. The few times he came always ended the same way. He would stir up a fight with me, and before I knew it, his bag was packed and he was screaming, "I don't know why I even bother to come over. You're such a bitch!"

By the end of the summer, James and I agreed that instead of returning to Phoenix, we would both stay in La Jolla for his senior year. I talked to Gerry about it and he didn't care one way or the other. He insinuated that I was "leaving" him. I just wanted a peaceful last year of high school for James instead of nightly battles. We enrolled him in La Jolla high school while I worked at the store. I made regular trips to Phoenix to transfer merchandise back to the La Jolla store. One day I flew from cool, sunny La Jolla to be greeted by the endless desert heat of Phoenix. It would turn into a day that changed my life. Gerry usually spent those hot months in La Jolla, but this year he decided to stay in Phoenix because he was planning a long European trip . . . without me. Strange, because after twenty years of marriage and always traveling as a twosome or family, he, who couldn't stand being alone, was going "alone."

Or was he?

FOURTEEN

Gerry Gets What He Deserves

The Blond Bimbo

When I arrived at CAPRICCIO that summer morning at the Borgata of Scottsdale, I was greeted by the familiar drip-drip of the fountain and strains of Vivaldi's Primavera playing over the music system. How I loved this store and the instant mood I felt every time I walked through the massive front doors! As soon as I was spotted, the salesgirls all ran over to greet me with big smiles. "We miss you!" "When are you coming back?" "The store just isn't the same when you're not here!"

But there was something in the air, something not quite right. Even Barbara, my favorite salesperson, gave me a somewhat furtive glance.

"Is something going on I should know about?" I asked her.

"Oh, Ollie, yes there is," she moaned. "I'm so glad you're here! Go ask Hilal. Talk to Hilal!" Hilal was our store manager, Gerry's son-in-law, and best friend. I pressed on.

"Barbara, is something wrong? Please tell me."

Before she could answer, I noticed across the room a young girl with long blonde hair, a mini skirt, and very tight sweater. "How did she get in the store? We're not open yet." I asked.

"Oh, Ollie, she's our new salesperson, Margaret Stone. None of us can stand her!" Barbara was getting nervous.

"Who hired HER? She doesn't look like she belongs here!" I was beginning to get annoyed.

"I know, I know, Ollie, but it was Gerry who hired her straight from the lingerie department at the Broadway." Barbara finally let it out.

I rushed back into Hilal's office, determined to get to the bottom of this, and confronted him with all the fury I was feeling. "What is going on with that blonde bimbo out there and Gerry?" I exploded! "I know something's up! What is it? She doesn't belong in this store and I want her out of here! We hire women with a little more refinement!" My voice was getting louder and louder.

"Calm down, Ollie. You're dreaming. Nothing, nothing is going on!" he replied a little nervously.

I continued. "Hilal, for the second time, what is going on between those two? I know you're lying, but I want to hear it from your own lips. If you don't tell me, I'll get on the loudspeaker and announce to everybody that Margaret is sleeping with my husband, and I want her out of this store!" By now I was screaming.

That threat and the tone of my voice must have scared him. He finally backed down and admitted, "Ollie, it's true. He's been seeing her for a long time. He took her to the polo matches in Palm Desert last weekend and he's planning to take her to Europe in a few weeks. He made me hire her."

The blood drained from my face. I felt as though I'd been instantly re-programmed, and I turned into a mad woman obsessed with getting to the bottom of this. "Hilal," I spewed out through tense lips, "I'm going home to confront Gerry about this. The bastard will probably deny everything. While I'm gone, you'd better get rid of that girl. Fire her! Personally escort her out of here! I want her gone by the time I return to the store." The anger was building. I grabbed my purse and flew out the door.

That trip from the store to Twenty-Fourth and East Georgia where we lived was the worst and longest twenty minutes of my life. My brain was racing.

"Of course Hilal will have called Gerry to forewarn him I was on my way, and that I knew about the girl.".

"I'm sure Gerry was infuriated." I was talking to myself.

"Good!" Let him stew!" "How could he do this?" I felt as though I had turned into some kind of creature interested only in the "kill."

"Twenty years of marriage," I spit out, "Ten good years and ten bad."

He was drinking heavily these days and would pass out on the couch every night, usually after a screaming match with James or me. There was the time when, in a drunken rage, he threatened to hit me over the head with a bottle of red wine and at the last minute poured it over my head, instead ruining my new white cashmere sweater. And the night he locked me out of the house and refused to let me back in. It was difficult to be loving towards him while he was in a drunken stupor, snorting and snoring, smelling strongly of liquor. I had lost all respect for him. How DARE he now subject me to the ignominy of this affair!

My head was ready to burst by the time I reached home. He was sitting in the family room calmly reading the paper when I walked in. "How COULD you?" I screamed. "How could you do this! You're old enough to be her grandfather."

"What are you talking about?" he quietly replied.

"You know damn well what I'm talking about. The whole store is talking about you and the blonde bimbo with the boobs."

"Ollie, there's nothing going on. Absolutely nothing! Calm down. She's just someone I'm trying to help, like a protégé."

"Protégé, my foot," I bellowed. "At least have the decency to be honest with me! You must think I'm pretty stupid to believe you're interested in anything other than what's between her legs!"

"Don't be so vulgar, Ollie, and just listen to yourself. You sound like a miserable fishwife. Anyone would look elsewhere if he had to put up with your screeching accusations."

He knew how to push my buttons. I was infuriated! He's up to his old tricks, "a strong offense is the best defense." "With all I've tolerated," I hissed, "your drinking, your rages, your anger, depression, violence, jealousies, and now your infidelities, why do I stay in this marriage? Why?

The thought of you and that young girl is disgusting. Hilal told me she's only nineteen years old. Does she make you forget you're sixty-five?"

"She's a lovely girl," Gerry insisted, "and I don't like your insinuations. I'm retired now and want to spend my time painting and finding peace"

"Are you planning to take her with you on this long awaited European trip?" I'm still screaming.

"No, I'm not," he lied.

"Hilal said you were."

"He's lying!"

"I don't believe you!" "You had better make up your mind, it's me or the girl. If she goes to Europe with you, it's the end of our marriage!" With that, I left and drove back to the store.

Of course she went to Europe with him. I knew, because I went to the airport and saw her. I felt like such a sneak. It was the same when, shortly after my confrontation with Gerry, I found out where Margaret lived and drove over to her house to talk. We sat in my car in front of the house, and I begged her to stop her relationship with Gerry.

"What relationship? I don't have a relationship with him. Why would I? He's much too old for me."

I was ready to kick her lying, sneaky, tight little ass! Another time I hired a private detective to watch our house. I had visited for the weekend and left late afternoon for La Jolla. Gerry insisted he was through with the girl, but I knew instinctively he was lying. I was obsessed with knowing the truth. My detective called later that evening to tell me within twenty minutes of my departure, she drove up and spent the night. She left very early in the morning. It showed me how low I could stoop, but I had the truth.

I wondered if there had been other girls. Gerry obviously liked them young. Already, the humiliation was beginning to take hold. I also wondered how many customers knew about this. I certainly didn't like being the last to know. Over and over, I thought about the two of them together. In our house? Our bed? I eventually did find out that Gerry gave her some of my clothes. That made me very angry. Also, years later Cindy told me she walked in on the two of them in our bed when she arrived home early from visiting friends. I was on a buying trip in New York at the time.

I didn't know I could hurt so much. When Gerry and Margaret left for Europe, my head was so heavy with pain, I couldn't sleep. I couldn't stop thinking about the two of them sharing a trip that should have been ours. What happened? When did it come to this? Did I do something wrong? I managed to get through the first few weeks by working in the store where my mind was constantly occupied. However, at night, all alone, I would lie awake hour after hour with my head buzzing from the weight of it all.

I began to realize that even with my success in business, I felt less than I would have been without a husband or partner in my life. I needed a man to make me feel good about myself. I had always been strong and self reliant, but it finally dawned on me that was all about business. This was my personal life and all about feelings I couldn't control: fear, anger, hurt, jealousy, depression, humiliation, confusion, powerlessness. I absolutely could not stop obsessing. The next morning, bleary-eyed from lack of sleep, I would put on my daytime persona and go to work.

About a month and a half went by, and one evening the phone rang. It was Gerry calling from Avignon, France.

"Ollie, it's me, Gerry. I miss you. Can you ever forgive me?"

I was surprised to hear from him, although I half suspected something would happen. Gerry continued, "Margaret and I are through! She's on her way back to the States now. I wondered if you would like to fly over for a couple of weeks and drive through the wine country with me."

I didn't know what to say. Since Margaret had come into our lives, I had such a deep and overwhelming love for Gerry I could think of nothing else but reconciliation. I forgot all about his drinking and his rages. This was different.

"I love you, Ollie, and only you. Margaret was a mistake and I want to make it up to you," he whispered softly. "Please come."

I was mesmerized. His charm would always get me, even though I knew it was his masterful manipulation at work. "Gerry, I don't know what to tell you. This comes as a surprise. Let me call you after I've looked at my schedule." I managed to not communicate my elation.

Suddenly, everything was all right. He was back and we would be together again. The girl was out of the picture. Gerry loved ME! Right then I should have told him to move out of the house. He had made his choice and I was not it. But I still loved him, or thought I did, and couldn't, achingly couldn't, say no. It was many years later I realized it wasn't love that held us together at all. Real love is based on respect and trust. What held us together was NEEDINESS. Gerry needed me for my strength. I needed Gerry for his support.

The phone call from Gerry was just what I needed. I was deliriously happy again. All was well. (How could I be so naïve!) I made plane reservations immediately, cleared my calendar, and started packing. I called Gerry the following day and told him I was coming. He was overjoyed, like the old Gerry I remembered. Within forty-eight hours I was on the plane to France.

Gerry met me at the airport, and after long hugs and kisses, we were on our way to the hotel. We only spent one night there. I felt slightly strange that only two nights ago he had been with Margaret probably in the same room, the same bed. I asked no questions. The following morning we left for our adventure on the road. We made no advance reservations and just stopped at the end of the day at small hotels along the way. I noticed Gerry was very quiet as we drove through the countryside. It was almost uncomfortable and not at all like him. He was usually outgoing and very talkative, which made me wonder if he was thinking about *her*. Several nights passed with very little affection and I began to regret making the trip. He was somewhere else. By the time we reached the outskirts of Paris, we had a major fight. He was furious that I asked him why he was so unhappy. Instead of reassuring me, he made me feel I had no business questioning his feelings.

"There you go again, Ollie. You haven't changed one bit. You think you know it all. Well, you don't. I can't stand this. I'm sorry I asked you to come all this way."

I could see it coming: He was trying to force a fight so I would join the screaming and he could justify running off. At that moment, it suddenly hit me! Why didn't I see it before? It wasn't Gerry who kicked the girl out. It was the girl who left him! She must have handed him some strong emotional blackmail, trying to force him to divorce me and marry her. He couldn't face that quite yet.

The following morning, after not speaking to each other all evening, we went to the airport together. Waiting for departure, we didn't speak. Once on board he sat in the back of the plane, alone. It was crazy, totally childish. When we finally reached Phoenix, the tension between us was ready to snap. He went his way and I went my way. We met at home. He slept in the guest bedroom that evening. In the morning he announced he was leaving and would start packing his things. I felt like a ping pong ball batted back and forth. Glad to see him go. Don't leave me. What do you see in her? You need me! Why? Why not? I was swept up in the misery of it all! I didn't know he had already rented a little love nest in Scottsdale, and that's where he was headed.

It didn't hurt quite so much the second time, because I was resigned to the reality of the breakup. The first thing I did was change all the locks. I knew Gerry would come to the house and remove what he wanted before any legal settlement. He still managed to break in a couple of times and denied taking anything. It was so petty. He came almost every day for a week and removed his belongings. He then asked if he could leave the balance of his stuff until he returned from a month-long trip. Was this the Antarctica trip? Australia? Ireland? What did it matter now. I would have loved to travel on those adventures with Gerry, but he never spoke to me about it. Margaret must have bathed him in the Fountain of Youth!

About a month later, Gerry surprised me by walking into my office with coffee and a croissant. He used to do this when he still worked at the store.

"Are you back from your trip already? " I asked.

"Oh, yes," he replied, "but I just wanted you to know it's definitely all over with Margaret. We had a number of fights on the trip, so I decided to return ahead of time. You were so right about her." I couldn't believe he was saying this.

"I'd like to come home. I miss you. You can't imagine how much I miss you. "He was almost pleading. I was beginning to feel like a mother to a wayward son, not a wife to a cheating husband.

I knew I should tell him to pack up the rest of his stuff and move out permanently, but I just couldn't do it at that point.

"Let me take you out to dinner tonight before you say no," he quickly asked. "I have so much I want to tell you."

It was a strange and insidious spell he had over me. Why couldn't I say no? I wanted him back so desperately, I was incapable of saying no. Did I fear being on my own? Yes, I was scared to death of being without him. What was the nature of my weakness? I was only thinking of our "good times" together, like those trips to art museums where he would explain a painter's technique or driving together in Ireland, France, or Italy. I didn't like being alone, but it was more about losing him to someone else that frightened me. I honestly felt he made me more interesting just by being there. It wasn't just fear of loneliness. It was the greater fear of missing out on the fullness of life together. He was exciting, charming, beguiling, and I wanted him back so badly I overlooked the infidelity and insanity. I pushed aside trust and respect. I thought I still loved him and my heart was full of forgiveness.

As the words slowly curled off my tongue, "All right, Gerry," I felt like a weak, pathetic, wimp! Dammit! This was the third time I took him back.

He came home with me that night, and started moving back a few days later. I felt as though some invisible force was controlling me, beckoning me to reconcile permanently. That sounded good to me, but deep down where I had buried all those bad memories, unsettling thoughts kept erupting. Gerry had not changed. He still drank heavily. He couldn't stop, and he needed help. He skirted the subject whenever I brought it up, but at this point he was watching how much he drank. It was like living in a bubble, praying it wouldn't burst too soon. I couldn't shake the feeling something was going to happen. But when?

Gerry invited me over to see the condo he and Margaret had shared and to help him pack. It felt very strange, because I couldn't shake imaginary thoughts of the life they shared there. As we walked around the rather small, dreary rooms, I thought of those painful memories and was almost physically sick. We sat in the kitchen, had a cup of coffee and talked. How he could talk! He told me about the trip and the events leading up to their "final" breakup. Once again he smothered me with verbal love, and once again I was mesmerized. He wanted to go back to Europe with me, to make up for the last unfinished trip. This time he suggested the South of France, maybe rent a villa for a month, and just get away together. The thought occurred to me that he had been running away for years now, running away from himself. Only now he wants me to join him in the flight.

"Why not?" I said in an enthusiastic voice, "I love the South of France!"

"Then it's settled," he replied," let's leave as soon as we can."

Gerry was always compulsive like that. I was ready for a vacation. I picked up a couple of books on the area and planned an itinerary for us. We made plane reservations, and everything was set to go in three days. The following afternoon Gerry called me at the store and asked to meet me at the condo. There was something he wanted to tell me, privately, with no one else around.

"Okay," I said, "I'll be there in a half hour."

The condo was only a few blocks away from CAPRICCIO. I couldn't imagine what was on his mind. He was standing in the doorway when I arrived, as though he couldn't wait to tell me the news.

"Let's sit here in the kitchen," he said, looking a little distraught.

"What's going on, Gerry? Is anything wrong?" I asked.

"Ollie, I'm so sorry, but we'll have to call off the trip to France," he said sheepishly. "Margaret is pregnant!" I was speechless. "Of course," he added, "I'll have to marry her." How absolutely foolish he sounded.

"But, Gerry," I said in as even a tone as I could, "You're already married to me!"

That was the final blow. There was no returning home now. Once again Gerry took all his belongings and moved back into the little condo with Margaret. They stayed in Scottsdale long enough to organize their big move up to Oregon. Our divorce was delayed until we agreed to a property settlement satisfactory to both of us. Overnight I turned into the enemy and Gerry the aggressor. We would never again speak quietly and gently with one another. From now on it was, "Who would get what?" It was lawyer time, and there were endless issues of "community property." Gerry's daughters, Joan and Nancy, were drawn into depositions that turned ugly and mean. I couldn't believe some of the things that were said. Their reality was so different from mine.

Most of the legal papers took months to finalize. We had all our property "in joint tenancy with right of survivorship," and we agreed to sell at a price no lower than a certain amount. We would split all proceeds half and half. We couldn't agree on which parcels of land in Carefree and Sedona were most valuable, so we didn't outright give this one to Ollie, and that one to Gerry. If either of us died before all the land was sold, the remainder would reasonably go to the survivor. It all seemed very logical at the time, but we hadn't considered the role of fate in our well made plans.

A few months after arriving in Oregon, Gerry had a serious stroke and Margaret gave birth to their baby daughter. I imagined the following scenario. Gerry, now in his late sixties, is on a stretcher in the hospital being wheeled in one direction for the doctors to operate on him. Margaret, in her early twenties, is being wheeled in the opposite direction to give birth to their child. It would make a touching moment for a TV show or movie.

Gerry had moved to Oregon to "get away." I lost track of him during the few years he lived there, and it didn't surprise me when I heard he was moving back to Arizona. He had undergone heart surgery and had a stroke while there. Gerry and Margaret finally married in 1989 after our divorce was final; then she left him and moved to the Midwest. Gerry sold his house, purchased another in Carefree, and resumed his painting.

A few months later, he was rushed to the hospital after another serious stroke. He lived alone but somehow managed to get to a phone and called for help. At the hospital, it was decided he would need long term care, and he was transferred to a hospice for the terminally ill. He stayed there in a state of semi-helplessness until his death about six months later. I never talked to him again before he died.

It was tragic that he spent so much time in a coma after his last stroke, but he died quietly in the hospice at the age of seventy-five on September 25, 1995. James and Cindy flew down to Phoenix for the funeral. It was like a scene from a movie. There I was, the second wife. And there she was, the third wife. Gerry's first wife had died. His four children ranged in age from six-year-old Elizabeth to forty-five year old Joan. In between was forty-two year old Nancy and twenty-eight year old James. Cindy, thirty-four, was not Gerry's daughter, but she had lived with him as her step-father for fifteen years.

 Most of our staff at CAPRICCIO attended his funeral services. It was a lovely, simple service with a large portrait of Gerry (painted by Gerry) on an easel in front of the room. The place was full of people who had known Gerry. Finally, Margaret and daughter arrived, walked down the aisle grand entrance style, and sat up front. Joan and Nancy gave their speeches, and so did Margaret. During all this I started crying. I wanted to get up and speak the whole truth about Gerry McNamara.

I wanted to talk about how we met and fell in love back in 1965. How kind and loving Gerry had been in those early years. How dashing and handsome he was. What fun we had as a family traveling to Jackson Hole, Wyoming, Sun Valley, Idaho, and the cruise through the Greek Islands. I remembered old friends like Linsley and Peter Haffenreffer from Bangor, Maine, whom we visited there and in Bermuda. I loved our time together, driving throughout Ireland even though it rained almost every day. There was always a special something about traveling with Gerry. When we were in County Clare, Ireland, we discovered it was the McNamara county.

When we told the head of the McNamara castle we were visiting that we were McNamaras, we were whisked up to the Royal Seating places and treated like royalty, complete with a four-course dinner, on us, of course.

But most of all I remember our trips driving through France and Italy. We always brought a tape player and had music along the way. I remember how I loved listening to Vivaldi's Primavera and leaning on Gerry's shoulder. Those were the Good Years. (More tears!)

And then the Bad Years crept in, quietly at first but like a time bomb ready to explode.

Alcohol took over and controlled him. He was mean, self-centered, and arrogant. He treated me as though I had no feelings. He expected me to understand his moods, his constant anger, his resentments. He would erupt instantaneously, screaming loudly with no control. With each year it became worse. By the time he found Margaret, I was another person. I didn't like me and what had become of me. But I didn't like what had become of Gerry even more.

Suddenly, I was brought back to the funeral by the sound of Margaret's voice. "And I couldn't believe how Gerry, defying his age, flew down to Antarctica just to see the penguins with me."

Margaret was painting her version of him now. She went on and on like Miss Goody-Two-Shoes with her own imaginary world-with-Gerry. She said nothing about leaving him for good because she couldn't cope with his impossible behavior from drinking anymore. She gave him what Gerry feared most of all in life, being alone and dying alone.

I often think about those years, and after living with Gerry for over twenty years, I felt I knew him better than anyone. Yet, I didn't know him at all. He missed his true calling in life, fulfilling his passion to be a great artist. He wasn't given that gift, the talent to paint like a Vermeer or Holbein, bestowed on only the few by an elusive God. Gerry would often say, with intense belief, that "only art endures." He spent his life frustrated by the reality that his paintings would never hang in the great museums.

Instead, he turned to other creative projects. Building our Borgata store, our La Jolla building, and filling the walls with his own paintings kept him busy for a few years. Once these were completed, he searched for something else to "fix" him. This time it was another woman, a move to Oregon, and his tireless search for peace.

"I want peace," he would repeat, "I want peace."

I didn't speak at Gerry's funeral. I walked out feeling very sad and wished I had had the courage to say something. I couldn't help thinking, "Maybe he's finally found peace." I returned to the store with that thought and the reality that it was finally over.

I didn't mourn for Gerry. Instead, I felt an enormous sense of relief. Now I could go on with my life with no more hurtful surprises from him.

Having spent almost a third of my life with Gerry and giving birth to our son, it was inevitable that memories would continue to pop up. Near the end, he and James would talk by phone about politics and current events. James loved talking to his dad long distance and missed it when he died. Cindy had bravely forgiven Gerry for his actions towards her, knowing she needed to do that for herself. She was never close to him. It was impossible to be close to Gerry. He had shut down parts of his inner self, and I'm convinced he did that at a very young age. That's why it was so difficult to reach him. He was much better with surface issues.

I would often ask him, "Why do you react so violently when I say something that upsets you?" Instead of an answer, he would lash back at me about my insensitivity and selfishness.

"Why," I would ask, "are you so negative about so many different people?" "How do you feel when the New York store insists you do something you disagree with?"

His answers to questions like these were always explosive. He could never see his part in the process as a negative one. It was always your fault or their fault. He was never to blame. At the end it didn't matter. He was gone, but all the mixed-up memories of our life together continue to haunt me in the middle of the night as

I thrash around in my bed screaming incoherently at the darkness. I never know when he will reappear.

How I wish he would go away.

FIFTEEN

Saint Peter

"Take off Your Clothes"

In 1988, when Gerry finally picked up the remainder of his belongings at the house, we said our reserved goodbyes. I never thought that would be the last time we would see each other, yet seven years later he was dead. During that same time I was busy with the store, keeping in touch with Cindy and James, and developing a romantic relationship with Peter Kruidenier.

I first met Peter in Phoenix when we both lived there. He was married to Liz, and we would occasionally see each other at friends' homes. I hardly knew him, but years later he divorced and moved to Newport Beach, California. When I was in the midst of all the turmoil of Gerry's affair with Margaret. I talked to my friend, Linda Samuel, who also had left Phoenix to live on the coast.

"Linda, I can't believe this is happening. The girl is only nineteen! Gerry's sixty-five! It's humiliating. How can it last? What can I do? He is really difficult to live with and drinks far too much, but I've always thought I could 'change' him. How can I get him back? Have I lost him for good?" I was sobbing throughout.

"Ollie, face it, the guy's a drunk, and you deserve better. You're lucky to be rid of him. Maybe you should talk to a friend of mine who lives here in Newport Beach. I know he spent five weeks in an alcohol rehabilitation center and attends a lot of AA meetings. He might be able to give you some insight into Gerry's behavior. He lived in Phoenix for about twenty years until he moved to the coast." Linda sounded so concerned and anxious to help, her voice alone gave me hope. "His name is Peter Kruidenier," she continued, "and I'm sure you two bumped into each other at some of the parties in Scottsdale."

"Of course I've met Peter." I said. "He was married to Liz for years. I didn't know he was divorced."

"He married a second time and moved to the California," Linda continued. "He then divorced her and became one of the most eligible bachelors in Newport Beach. He told me I was too young for him, so instead we became good friends. I think you two definitely should meet again." Linda gave me Peter's number and the following evening I called.

"Hello, Peter, this is Ollie McNamara calling from Phoenix. Do you remember me?"

"Ollie, of course I remember you. How's Gerry? What's going on in Phoenix?" He sounded friendly enough, approachable, and mildly curious.

"Linda Samuel gave me your number, and after listening to me for about an hour she suggested I call you. Peter, I really need help. Over the last few years Gerry has been drinking more and more heavily, passing out on the couch, and behaving erratically with abrupt mood swings. Now he's decided to leave me for a nineteen-year-old girl and I'm totally lost. At first I thought he was joking, because for months he denied any involvement. Last week he packed up his clothes and told me he was leaving. He was through with the marriage. By the time I finished my story, I was sobbing. "What should I do, Peter, what should I do? I love him and don't want to lose him."

"It's the best thing that ever happened to you, Ollie." Peter was jubilant. "It's a true blessing in disguise. You don't see that now, but it's giving you an opportunity to have a life. He's a drunk and you shouldn't be wasting your time trying to get him back. Be glad he's gone."

"But, Peter," I wailed, "I love him. I can't bear the thought of losing him. How can you be so heartless?"

"Ollie, the guy's sick," Peter continued. "He's an alcoholic and my advice to you is forget about him. You can't change him; only he can do that. And he's not about to change. Therefore, you've got to change yourself if you're going to survive this."

"How can you be so cruel, Peter," I was soaked with heart-wrenching tears. "I looove him. I missssss him. I want him baaaaack. I called you for help, and is that all you have to say? Forget about him?"

"That's right," Peter repeated. "Forget about him."

With that I slammed down the receiver. I was so angry. How could he be so heartless? I wanted sympathy and understanding, not this cold, bare attitude of black and white. I was sorry I'd called him.

A week went by. Two weeks. I was waterlogged with self-pity by now and felt alone and desolate. I had half-expected Peter to call me back to apologize and tell me what I wanted to hear. But not this Peter. Not this recovering-alcoholic, I-know-my-program Peter. Not this rigorously-honest-daily-meeting-Peter. So I called him, again.

This time our conversation was less emotional. I told him how few people I knew who understood about changing themselves in order to find peace. I also shared with him that a friend of mine suggested I attend some Alanon and Alcoholics Anonymous meetings. I called their main offices to inquire about meetings and found out the time and place for that evening. I picked up a schedule for both programs there, but that was just the beginning. I didn't know what to expect and was pleasantly surprised to discover how honest and sincere everyone was about sharing their stories. I learned simply by listening.

"Ollie," Peter said, "you're doing all the right things. I wish I could talk to you directly, face to face, but I have no plans to visit Phoenix in the near future."

"That's okay," I said, "I'll be visiting the La Jolla store next week. Maybe you can drive down and we can get re-acquainted."

We made plans to have our first date the following week when I flew over. By now the shock of Gerry's leaving me was not so extreme, and though we were officially separated, our divorce wasn't final until early 1989. I was learning to live one day at a time, although at first it was one minute at a time and then one hour. It was a pleasant change to look forward to something again.

I flew to San Diego a week later. It was always breathtaking to fly over the mountains and descend with the Pacific Ocean beneath me. I never tired of that view. It was much cooler than Phoenix when I arrived, something I welcomed. The store was bustling with customers, so I gave our manager a wave hello and went upstairs to the apartment. After dropping off my things, I went down to spend the day in the store.

That evening Peter was expected at seven o'clock. I was a little nervous when he hadn't arrived by seven-thirty. I thought he might have been hurt or was standing me up. Just then the phone rang and it was Peter, somewhat upset, because he had been rear-ended on the freeway. His car was hit by a speeding truck with such force that it spun him around until he stopped on the center divide danger-ously facing oncoming traffic from the opposite direction. Luckily, no one was hurt. The police were there in minutes, turned Peter's car around, and instructed him to follow them off the busy Fri-day-night, traffic-filled freeway. Since the car was badly damaged, Peter was amazed it was still drivable. Once safely off the road, the police questioned him about the hit-and-run vehicle, filled out some forms, and left. Peter then called to tell me about the accident and to let me know he was going to continue on to La Jolla. Hopefully, the car would make it.

Peter arrived about an hour later, still somewhat shaken by the accident. His beautiful Mercedes was a mess, but the engine hadn't been touched. I invited him upstairs to the apartment, but it was almost nine o'clock, so we left immediately for dinner at Avanti's. He was as handsome as ever, six feet tall with thinning hair and an irresistible smile. But it was his extraordinary voice with per-fectly tuned words that I noticed the most. We had so much to talk about, and as we ate dinner I knew this was just the beginning. I was instantly attracted to him, and found myself talking less and less about Gerry and more and more about Peter.

"How long have you lived in Newport Beach?" I asked.

"About two-and-a-half years," he answered. "My lease is up in six months, and I was planning to move to San Diego to live with Dick Sorel, an old friend from Phoenix."

"I know Dick. He and Toni used to have the best parties. I'm sure we bumped into each other at one of them," I said with my early-in-the-relationship tone of voice.

That night I wore a skinny black leather skirt with a filmy white blouse. At the last minute I pinned on a beautiful pink silk rose. Peter insinuated I was hiding behind that rose, and to this day he still teases me about hiding my face in it. I think we were the last people to leave the restaurant, and as we drove home Peter asked when we could get together again.

"I usually spend July and August in the La Jolla store," I said, "but maybe I'll spend June as well this year."

"Good idea," Peter replied. "It's an easy drive down from Newport Beach."

When we arrived home, Peter politely shook my hand at the door and said he would see me soon. I was a little disappointed he didn't give me a hug or a kiss, but as I went up to the apartment, I waved goodbye from the upper terrace. I knew he would call.

The following day I flew back to Phoenix. It was early May, 1988, and the extended summer heat was just beginning. In another week I would be in New York on a buying trip already planned for this time. When Peter called, I told him I would be gone for about ten days. He then came up with the idea of my flying to Newport Beach, spending the weekend there, and continuing on to New York. At first it sounded crazy, but he kept trying to persuade me. Before the call was finished he had convinced me to do just that. What was the matter with me, going West to go East?

During that week Peter called every day. We talked about my two children, his two children, my work, his family, Iowa, Cornell, Auburn, and by the time I boarded that airplane, I felt I'd known him forever. Something was happening between us. I couldn't wait to see him, and when I arrived at the John Wayne airport he gave me that charismatic smile again. At that moment I knew he felt the same way I did.

It was mid-morning and I hadn't eaten a thing, so Peter took me to a small restaurant along the way to his place. As we sat in the booth eating, I was very aware of his body turned towards mine and his gaze riveted on my eyes. We played with small talk until we finished eating, and then drove to his apartment overlooking the end of the bay. He had a magnificent view of boats coming and going. I sat looking out at the boats when Peter came to join me. I thought we would take a walk or continue to sit there looking at the boats. Instead Peter stood towering over me for a moment, then leaned over with both arms on the couch on either side of my head, his face about two inches away from mine, and looked directly at me.

"Take—off—your—clothes," he ordered.

"Take off my clothes? Now?" I stammered. I was not used to this.

"Yes. NOW," he repeated.

He took me by the hand and led me to his bedroom. By now half my clothes were on the hallway floor. As we undressed, he mentioned he had a water bed. I'd never been on a water bed before, and when I lay down I felt like I had been dropped on a pile of giant marshmallows. I bobbed up and down totally out of control of my body and, laughing hysterically, felt like a three-year-old with a new toy. Then Peter jumped in, all one hundred eighty-five pounds of him, and I half expected the mattress to split like an old, tired mass of bubble wrap. But it didn't, and soon Peter had everything under control. He was a master on the water bed.

SIXTEEN

Cindy and James

The Children Grow Up

After that weekend and my trip to New York, I was busy writing orders and planning an early summer in La Jolla. I missed Peter, but we talked every night by phone. Business was slowing down as we approached June and the beginning of a long, hot, Arizona summer. I was looking forward to James spending time with me in La Jolla, since it would be his last summer before graduating.

James was now twenty-one and attending the San Francisco Art Institute, studying film and photography. He had spent one year in Europe on a program sponsored by the school and was required to bring back footage of his trip. He spent the first part of his project in Italy visiting Florence, Venice, and stops in between. He then flew to Paris to meet me while I was on a buying trip. He arrived looking like the traveling troubadour, with happy guitar flung over his back and jam-packed-backpack over his shoulder. He needed a shave and shower and some clean clothes. I had missed him so badly during the half year he was gone, I just threw my arms around him and hugged and kissed his grisly face.

"It's so good to see you, James. I've missed you so much. I love you so much." Kiss, kiss, kiss, kiss, kiss.

"Me too, Mom. How are you? Working too hard? Got lots to tell you." James was ever the charmer, and he was at his best that evening. After a much needed shave and shower, he looked pretty handsome. We sent a big load of laundry to see him through the balance of his trip to Barcelona, Spain.

That evening we celebrated our reunion over dinner. James told us about his travels and the people he'd met along the way. "I met some interesting people in Italy, Mom. I really liked Florence and took some great scenes with my new camera. Taking the train made traveling a lot easier. I'm so happy to see you again." He took my two hands into his, looked deeply into my eyes, and said, "I love you, Mom. Thanks for making this trip possible."

Three days later I finished my buying trip and left for home. James flew from Paris to Spain, spent several months enjoying himself there, and then returned to San Francisco. This would be his last year at the Art Institute. James graduated in 1989. Peter and I drove up for the ceremony. His father didn't attend.

"James," I said, "I'm sorry your Dad didn't come. I know it would have meant a lot to you."

"Mom, don't worry about Dad not being here. We knew he wouldn't come." James was always accepting of his father's actions. "I'm glad you came, though."

Peter and I spent a few days in San Francisco, sight-seeing, shopping, and planning dinner with James each evening. He knew some interesting places, like Julius Castle located on a hill overlooking the Bay. The dining was excellent; the view breathtaking.

I made a point of visiting James several times a year and on one trip in 1993 suggested he look for another apartment. He was living in the meat locker of an old warehouse, one tiny, claustrophobic room. There were no windows, and he received air in the room from a pipe leading up through the roof. He shared the bathroom and living room (formerly the drive-in entry to the warehouse). Worst of all he liked it! I never did understand that, and couldn't wait for the day he would move out.

Finally, weeks later, James called me in La Jolla and said he'd like to look for another place to live. I was thrilled he wanted to move and suggested he walk up and down streets of areas he liked looking for signs in the windows.

James on a rooftop in San Francisco when he was in his twenties

"It might not be a bad idea to look for a condo as well, since you say you want to stay in San Francisco indefinitely and rents are so high there."

"A condo? Wow. That's great." James was elated. "I'll start tomorrow. You never know when you'll see something."

I've never seen James so excited. The following week he called to report that he had decided Potrero Hill was the area he preferred. He had spent the entire week looking, and on the fifth day at about four o'clock noticed a sign in the window of a three story small building on Potrero Hill. "CONDO FOR SALE." James rang the doorbell and was buzzed in. The condo was on the third floor, and as he walked in the broker approached him, shook his hand, and showed him around the entire apartment. James was impressed by his courtesy, because he was self-conscious about his own appearance.

As they talked, James explained, "My mom is buying the condo for me. I'll call her tonight and maybe she'll come in the next day or two. I really like it."

When James called, full of enthusiasm and descriptions, I decided to fly up the following day. "I'd like to look at a few more condos while I'm up there, James. Maybe we shouldn't rush this."

"Wait till you see it, Mom. Just what you like. Light and airy, not dark and dreary like the place I'm in now. You walk into a little hall and into a nice living room with a fireplace. One wall has sliding glass doors that lead to a small outdoor patio. The continuing wall forms a window seat, and the area is used as a dining room. View of the Golden Gate bridge from the window seat is spectacular. The kitchen is next to it. The hallway leads to a bathroom and two bedrooms at the opposite end. One bedroom has an adjoining bathroom. I'll probably make one room my computer room. Each room has wall-to-wall windows. We see the Bay Bridge from these windows and a great view of downtown San Francisco. I love it."

I didn't waste any time and flew up the next day. I rented a car at the airport, picked up James, and drove to the condo at 116 Connecticut Street. We called ahead to make an appointment with Bob Wellenstein, the realtor who was going to show us the condominium. This was in December of 1993. James was right. It was very attractive, but expensive. I explained to Bob I was going to see several other places before making my decision.

"We'll be back later today after we've looked around," I remarked.

Three other places we saw that day weren't nearly as nice, and James didn't like the locations. I totally agreed, so we returned and talked to Bob. After negotiating, making a few calls, and talking to the owners, we bought the condo. Within a few weeks it was available for James to move into, so I flew up again to help him. I was more concerned about what not to take, because James couldn't bear to part with what he called treasures and I called junk. We managed to sort it all out, and the next step was buying a king size bed, end tables, and a chest of drawers.

It reminded me that only three years earlier on one of my trips to Fort Collins to visit Cindy, I casually asked if she would like to buy some land to build a house. Or did she have any interest in buying a house. "Aren't you long past the concrete-block-bookcase stage yet?" I asked. "And don't you need more than one small, stuffed, overflowing closet?"

It came as a surprise to her because she was renting a farmhouse with one of her horsey friends and was reasonably happy there. I suggested she keep an eye out for something in the future when she suddenly remembered. "I loved the place where I used to board my horses located on a hill overlooking the Rocky Mountains. I heard the owner just put it up for sale because she wanted to move back to Denver."

"Great!" I exclaimed, "Let's not waste any more time. Let's go there."

"Okay, Mom, but it's probably sold by now."

"Don't be so sure, Cindy. Why don't we drive over there and look. Do you know where it is?"

"It's in LaPorte, about a twenty-minute drive from Fort Collins." By now Cindy was beginning to realize I was serious.

"Let's go," I said. "This may be our lucky day."

As we drove off, Cindy couldn't stop talking about the place. She described it as a little ranch with stables for six horses, two large pastures, and a cozy house. She loved the area because it was very quiet with plenty of trees and land for horses to graze. It wasn't long before we reached the property, and we both saw the "For Sale" sign together.

"The house hasn't sold yet," screamed Cindy.

We were both excited, took down the realtor's information, and drove up to the house in case the owner or agent were there. They weren't, so Cindy showed me around the place, and as we left she said something that really touched me.

"Mom, is it really possible I might own this? It's like a dream come true."

Cindy contacted the agent as soon as we reached home, and they set up an appointment to meet the following afternoon. I left for Phoenix that morning. We discussed that she could handle it herself, negotiate the price, and then call me. That evening she phoned to tell me the owner accepted her much-lower-than-asking-price.

"Ask him if he can lower it even further for all cash," I advised.

Cindy called me the next morning, July 16, 1990 as the "proud owner of her very first house." They lowered the price another five thousand so she signed the sales agreement. As I arranged to wire the cash to Cindy, I was happy to know the house was hers free and clear and she was relieved of any mortgage payments.

Cindy moved in two weeks later after all the paperwork was cleared. I flew up to help her clean out the house in preparation for new wood floors to be installed. It was a labor of love as we threw out endless piles of leftover "stuff" and planned minor structural changes. We ate pizza delivered to the house and worked late into the night for days. We were exhausted. At one point I suggested to Cindy that she hire a professional decorator I had used in our homes in Phoenix and La Jolla.

"Would you like Patty Hasbrook or Theresa to fly up to help pull this place together?

"Oh, Mom, I'd love it," Cindy exclaimed. "I don't know where to begin with these empty rooms."

"Good," I said, anxious not to impose my ideas on her. "In the long run you'll avoid making mistakes and your home will look beautiful."

I returned to Phoenix but made several trips back to La Porte, Colorado to visit Cindy during the renovation. The floors were finally completed after we agonized over what color to stain the wood, and wallpapers, fabrics, and furniture had all been ordered when Theresa flew up to visit Cindy to discuss the project. It took about two months after her trip before everything was ready to be sent up from Phoenix to La Porte. On the Big Day the moving vans arrived with Cindy's entire house interior to be installed. Theresa arrived and Cindy was asked to leave for the day until the house was completely installed with draperies, paintings, and mirrors hung and all the furniture placed. Imagine Cindy's surprise at the transformation! I was home in Phoenix when she called, and the excitement in her voice said everything. She loved it.

SEVENTEEN

Cindy, I'm Your Father

Reuniting Father and Daughter

That same year, in 1990, Peter encouraged me to attend my fortieth Cornell class reunion in Ithaca, New York. It was a first for me, so we decided to explore campus between meetings and see all the changes that had taken place in forty years. I was surprised to see the number of new buildings that had been added but happy all the old familiar ones were still there. When we left after three days, there was a silent tug at my heart, because I had spent four happy years at Cornell and probably would not return again. As we drove away, I caught a final glimpse of the Tower Clock as it slowly disappeared into the familiar, sunlit background.

After the reunion, our next plan was a forty mile trip north to Auburn to see my high school English teacher, Catharine Parsell. I hadn't seen her in over twenty years. When we arrived, she came to the door to welcome us. I couldn't resist giving her lanky, six foot figure a big hug. She stood back, still looking like a female Ichabod Crane, and stared at me with disbelief.

"You're here. You're finally here. Come in," she smiled with a twinkle in her eyes. "I can't wait to get caught up with you. It's been much too long."

She was in her eighties now, having taught English at East High School until she retired, and as we sat in her living room sipping iced tea for at least two hours, she asked, "Ohlga," (She always pronounced my name with a hard "O.") you look very happy and relaxed. Peter must be a good influence on you."

"He is, Catharine. He's the best partner I've known and I'm very happy."

"And how about you, Peter. How do you feel?" Catharine was playing the mother.

"Catharine," Peter replied, "I love Ollie very much and intend to spend the rest of my life with her."

"Good," said Catharine. "Now I can rest in peace."

After lunch we tried to visit Ma and Pa's grave, but we couldn't find them in that huge graveyard. I did the next best thing. I stood under a big, beautiful tree and said some prayers. I couldn't help remembering what alcohol had done to my father and how sad it was that he seldom enjoyed his family. He was a true loner. We never could talk to him about his drinking. He would just laugh at us and say, "It's all right; it's all right." Even the rustling leaves whispered through the branches as we stood there, confirming all was well.

The following day we left Auburn and headed east for New England. After spending the night, we visited Amherst where Peter had attended college; then we decided to go to Nantucket Island. It was my first trip there, but it reminded me of all the trips I used to take to Cape Cod when I lived in New York City. I can still hear those honking seagulls. We stayed for three days and came home with the two beautiful oil paintings of children playing at the beach that now hang in my home.

When we planned this trip, I thought about trying to find Cindy's birth father, John Wright, on Shelter Island on the tip of Long Island where he used to own a home. In the twenty-six years since our divorce, her father never contacted her, never sent a birthday card nor a letter. Cindy knew Gerry was not her birth father because I told her, but she never asked about her "real daddy." In many ways it was easier to raise her without conflict. Now, however, I felt it was time to let her decide whether she wanted to see him again or not.

It was a long shot, but after a few phone calls we located Dick Edwards, John's best friend, and were told Dick was on Shelter Island for the summer. I was getting excited about reaching the island and talking to Dick, hoping we would find him there. We drove to the end of Long Island to Greenport and boarded the ferry, and as we drove off heading into town, memories of all those years began to return. John's house was situated on the water, and Cindy used to play in the sand with her little bucket and shovel. John used to fly in from New York and buzz the house to let us know he had arrived. The town was very small, and as we drove by a few buildings, I recognized the only bar there. How could I forget; John spent so much of his time there.

"Peter, look, there's Dick's bar. Shall we stop now or explore the island first?" I was curious to know if he was there.

"It's up to you, Ollie, but I'd suggest getting the island out of your system. Let's explore first and then come back." Peter was curious too.

We circled the small island and through the help of neighbors, found John's house. Unfortunately, it had been sold many years before. We decided to return to town and try to find Dick. We were told the bar in town was called "Dick Edwards" and that he was usually there. Maybe we would be lucky. As we ambled in we noticed a solitary man sitting at the bar. He was hunched over, with both elbows on the bar, drinking beer. He never looked up to see who had entered. Instead, he sat staring blankly ahead remaining in his own little world.

I tapped him on the shoulder and asked hesitatingly, "Hi, are you Dick Edwards?"

"Sure am," he replied. "Who are you?"

"I'm Ollie, remember me? Years ago I was married to your best friend, John Wright."

"Ollie? Ollie? Ohhhh, Ollie! Sure, I remember you. What are you doing here?"

He never got up from his barstool to greet me with a handshake or a hug. He just turned his head and stared. Peter and I stood there next to his bar stool and continued our conversation with Dick.

"Dick, is John still alive, and if so where can I reach him? Our daughter, Cindy, is twenty-nine now and lives in Fort Collins, Colorado. She's never seen nor heard from him since we left in 1965."

"My God, Ollie, what a surprise!" he exclaimed. "John lives in the Cayman Islands now. He's remarried and occasionally returns to Shelter Island."

"That's wonderful news. Can you please give me John's phone number and address as well as yours? I'll give them to Cindy and she can decide what to do about contacting him. She doesn't know I'm doing this, but at least she'll have a choice." After exchanging information, Peter and I left Shelter Island to drive back to New York.

We flew home the following day, and I immediately called Cindy to tell her about our contacting Dick Edwards. I gave her the phone number and told her it was all up to her now. She was really surprised and kept Dick's phone number for several months before calling. When she finally did, he gave her John's address as well. In August, Cindy wrote a long letter to her dad, but she didn't mail it until December. In the letter she wanted to know if he wanted a relationship or not and asked him to let her know one way or the other.

He replied and also tried to call. He checked with the City of Fort Collins for Cindy Wright's phone number and eventually they reached one another. After a long conversation, John told Cindy he would send her round trip tickets to Grand Cayman for her birthday the following month.

She was very excited about meeting him and discovering her father was an outdoorsy person like her. On that trip they hiked and snorkeled and swam day after day. Cindy made a second trip a year later and told her father the good news. She was getting married to Grant Jones in September, 1993, and wanted him to attend. Grant and Cindy met at work. He had been married once before and had two children, a daughter, Willow, and a son, Eli. The romance blossomed quickly, and he soon proposed.

John was happy to be asked. "Wouldn't miss it for the world," he said, "I'm the father of the bride!"

Nothing would have made Cindy happier. She called me in Phoenix and asked if I would help her plan the wedding, and told me she was determined to find the most beautiful outdoor location in Colorado. She finally did. While riding horses with Grant at the Two Bar 7 Ranch on the Colorado-Wyoming border, they located the perfect setting for their celebration. It was a mountain meadow framed by endless glistening aspen, a small lake, and a thirty foot wall of natural rock.

"This is it!" Cindy exclaimed with joy. "This is exactly what I wanted to find!"

Once that was decided, we spent days on all the details of the caterer, the wedding cake, the florist, the menu, the music, and on and on. The logistics of planning an outdoor wedding where everything must be brought to the site are mind boggling, particularly when you are miles from home, as we were. Can't forget anything.

The day of the wedding, the florist placed garlands and bouquets of flowers and streamers against the thirty-foot rock, forming a beautiful backdrop for the service. Chairs had been set up facing the "altar," and in the adjoining meadow, round tables and chairs were arranged for the wedding luncheon. It was a breezy early fall morning with sunshine and blue skies. Cindy had carefully selected favorite music to be played including "Vivaldi for Lovers." A friend sang "Give Yourself to Love" while the wedding party walked to the "altar."

It was nice to see Cindy and her father together. They were completely comfortable, and I was happy the long separation was over. It was obvious they adored each other. John had retired from King Features Syndicate and decided to live on Grand Cayman years before. As I watched them interact, I was satisfied I'd done my part. Cindy had found her real father at last. Grant, in his quiet way, endeared himself to me simply by loving Cindy. He was an honest, hard working man, and as he waited for Cindy and her father to arrive in their old horse and buggy, it was obvious he was very happy.

The wedding party was brought to the ceremony in two antique horse-driven carriages. The first, carrying the three bridesmaids, was a stagecoach covered with fresh flowers and led by two huge white and grey horses. Cindy and her father rode up behind them in an open buckboard wagon also laden with

The three bridesmaids were brought to the wedding in an antique stagecoach led by two huge white and grey horses

colorful flowers. As the group walked in pairs to the "pulpit," there was a momentary gasp when the guests first saw Cindy. She wore a spectacular wedding gown made for her in London by a young English designer who specializes in one-of-a-kind designs. It was made of white tissue silk brocade with puff sleeves to the elbows and beaded tight sleeves to the wrists. The entire bodice was heavily beaded in pale pink and white beads. Her voluminous, long skirt rustled and billowed as she walked with her father down the natural aisle. She looked like someone from the 1800s, fragile, vulnerable, and beautiful.

The ceremony was brief with Cindy and Grant exchanging vows. They were pronounced husband and wife, they kissed, and walked down the pathway with strains of Vivaldi wafting in the warm,

The bride and her father rode in an open antique buckboard wagon

autumn air. The following day the temperature dropped so drastically that it began to snow. We were ecstatic it waited a day.

James and Peter came to the wedding and made the day perfect for me. I spent a lot of time with James there; one of my favorite photos shows our backs to the camera with James' arm flung across my shoulder. We are looking at the guests in the meadow. As I briefly stared at John Wright sitting at one of the tables, I thought he looked much the same, but older and thinner.

Silently I whispered to myself, "Thank you, John, for flying up from Grand Cayman to give Cindy away. You made her so happy."

We didn't know then it would be John's last trip. A month or two after returning home, he was airlifted to Fort Lauderdale with a serious case of pneumonia. A month later it cleared up, but before releasing him from the hospital the doctors discovered he had lung cancer. Two months after her honeymoon, Cindy was told by Betsey how serious his cancer was. Cindy decided instantly to pack a bag and go to Fort Lauderdale. She was there as his cancer worsened, and she was by his bedside when he died a week later in December, 1993.

When I asked her what it meant to find her father after so many years, she simply said, "It wasn't only closure, Mom. It was more like discovering a piece of myself."

EIGHTEEN

Time out to Play

Happy Days Abroad

Meanwhile, I returned to work to find business was booming at CAPRICCIO. The eighties had been very good to us, and the Borgata was the place to shop. During these years, we had been approached to open a store in Biltmore Fashion Park in Phoenix, but I wasn't sure we needed two stores in such close proximity. Gerry was in Ireland at the time, and when I called him for advice, he didn't particularly like the idea. I asked him to think about it and to call me in the next few days. When he did call, he said he would be coming home the following day and we could discuss it further at that time. When he returned we decided to meet with the Biltmore developers, and after seeing the prime location they offered and the terms of the lease, we decided it would supplement our Borgata business. So we agreed to do it.

After the architects finished plans, the building began. Gerry was on location daily, and after almost a year it was finished. Unlike the Borgata store, which was very Italian, the Biltmore store was French in feeling. It was five thousand square feet compared to the Borgata's ten thousand, with pastel walls and light wood through-out. The ceilings were very high, giving an added roominess to the interior. We opened with a big party, inviting our clients and the press, and we received wonderful coverage in the newspapers the following few days. Our monthly full-page, color ads in *Phoenix* magazine would now include the Biltmore location.

There were three CAPRICCIO stores, and a fourth one was added a few years later in La Jolla at La Valencia Hotel. It was beautiful, but very small. The clients all wanted to go to the "big" store. It was a form of advertising on Prospect Street. We stayed there only three years, and though it broke my heart to close, we decided it was the best decision. The store was simply too small to do the volume we had expected.

Three stores were enough, requiring buying trips to Europe twice a year and to New York three times. In addition, I was busy with eight to ten fashion shows a year. They were all for charitable fund–raising, with a minimum of five hundred guests. Our biggest annual show was held in Tucson, Arizona for the Angel Charity for Children. It attracted almost eight hundred people and always ended up with standing room only and a waiting list. Over the fourteen years we did the show, the women from the charity managed to design stage settings equal to a smaller Broadway. They had the help of a retired New York stage designer who was very creative. One year the theme was the Paris Collections, so the stage became a street of French boutiques. Another year was an homage to Broadway, and they constructed a stage-wide set of stairs similar to staircases the Ziegfield Follies girls walked down. What a challenge to choreograph the models entering and exiting on different levels! The year they decided to do an Egyptian/Cleopatra theme, I was carried on stage in a litter by four bare-chested muscle men. It brought down the house, even though I almost tripped as I stepped down. The New York, New York theme was really exciting, with a stage background of the New York skyline and a dynamic opening to the song, " New York, New York, it's a wonderful town." My assistant and I planned the music, lighting, and choreography for each show, selected all the clothes and accessories, and did the lineup. A lot of work and time went into every show. CAPRICCIO absorbed all the costs as our contribution to the charity every year. I felt it was our thank you to the community.

The fashion business was my career for over fifty years, from 1950 to 2000. Most of that time was with Saks Fifth Avenue and CAPRICCIO. Owning our own stores was the high point, and from 1976 to 2000 we grew into fashion leaders in the industry. *Women's Wear Daily* described CAPRICCIO as "one of the ten most beautiful stores in America," and we were regularly singled out for current stories in local papers as well. I was driven to promote everything that related to the stores, and our immense success showed it. But as glamorous as the fashion business is, it still boils down to long hours and hard work. Early on, we decided our niche would be unusual clothing for the lifestyle of our customers. When I selected clothes to buy for the stores, I always kept that in mind. I avoided overly basic looks that were boring. If I bought classic, the fabric or the color had to make it exciting. Coordinated groups with a high fashion touch were the signature of CAPRIC-CIO. Our clients attended balls, dinner parties, and entertained at home. They shopped, lunched out, and went to the country club. They were always looking for a special gown or outfit for an important occasion.

Work took up most of my time, but by the late 1980s my personal life began to be important, and for the first time in years I took time out to "play." My divorce from Gerry was final in 1989, and at last I was free, unencumbered, and ready to make up for all those miserable years. Peter and I had been very discreet up to this point, but once Gerry was out of the picture we were ready to make some changes. We were very much in love and wanted to be together more. Peter had already decided to move from Newport Beach to San Diego, but instead of living with his friend Dick Sorel as planned, he moved in with me in La Jolla. Once again he asked me to marry him, but after my three unsuccessful marriages I didn't want to think of it. Instead, he moved in and we continued a strong, loving, understanding relationship. We did a lot of traveling early on, and I even invited him to come to Paris with me on one of my buying trips. He was impressed by the extravagant designer fashion shows, and he particularly liked the Emanuel Ungaro collection, because it was full of color. When I had my appointments to write orders, he went off to the Louvre or just walked the Paris streets, stopping for coffee and watching the people go by. In the evenings, we would find one of the many casual restaurants close by, and afterwards I worked frantically on orders required by my vendors before leaving Paris.

The following year, 1991, Peter and I decided to go on an African Safari to Kenya and Tanzania, ending the trip by traveling up the Nile in Egypt. What a memorable experience to take that long journey and land in a strange, unfamiliar world full of new sights, smells, and sounds! It appeared desolate and poor, with the natives dressed in colorful materials and walking barefoot on the dusty roads. On our first day we were taken out in jeeps to the plains where the animals lived. There were six in our group, all in Africa for the first time. We were awed by the endless numbers of animals; spotting a lion attack and kill a little gazelle, rip it open, and eat it, left us speechless. We saw tigers, elephants, giraffes, and learned from our native guide that they travel in groups like a family: mother, father, children, cousins. When one is singled out for the "kill," it's a member of a family that is lost.

It was the wildebeests that fascinated me. They look like small buffalo and form a constant, single, endless row of running animals. They never stop. Even when giving birth, the mother stops momentarily, tries to start the young animal running, and is off with the herd again. We learned that it is difficult to spot leopards because they are nocturnal, but on our last day we finally saw our first and only leopard, gracefully and silently stalking its prey. What a moment!

At camp we slept in individual tents on relatively comfortable cots. The first night I peeked outside to see endless black, and all I could hear were animal noises. I thought they were just outside our tent, because they grew louder and louder as I lay quietly on my bed. I was terrified.

"Peterrrrr," I moaned. "I'm scared. Are you scared? Can I come over to your cot to make me feel better?"

"You're in Africa, Ollie," he said without a hint of consolation. "Go to sleep. I'll see you in the morning. This cot isn't big enough for me alone, much less with you."

I did get through that night, only to be greeted the next morning with a pot banging to announce that our shower water was ready.

It was cold outside; as I gingerly tip-toed over to the shower tent, I didn't know what to expect. There I was, shivering in Africa, totally naked, and a booming voice on the other side commanded me to pull the cord. The cord was attached to a pail of water, my allotment, and I stood underneath the pail as I pulled and the water poured down on me. It was heavenly, warm water. It was also the fastest shower I'd ever taken. After dressing, with my teeth chattering non-stop, we went to breakfast in the master tent. They put on a feast, and we were given plenty of choices, like cereals, eggs and bacon, muffins, fresh fruit, toast, and coffee. Our safari lasted only six days, and when it ended we were all sad to leave.

Our next adventure was traveling up the Nile on a comfortable boat filled with tourists from different countries. We stopped along the way to see points of interest like the big dam at Aswan and the great statues of Ramses II. We also stopped at Luxor, the great Temple of Karnak, and on the opposite side, the burial site of the great pharaohs, including King Tutankhamun. Everyone on the journey was fascinated by this ancient history, but we had our lighter moments as well. One evening we were told there would be a costume party the following night, and we could purchase local Egyptian clothing at the bazaar in town where our next stop would be. We all wanted to outdo each other, so with great enthusiasm Peter and I wandered through the streets of the shopping bazaar looking for something spectacular. I ended up with a bright turquoise and silver caftan-like piece with a head scarf to match, and Peter found a white caftan that looked more like a sheet with a rope to tie around his waist. The night of the party, the room was filled with bazaar sampling. Everyone was in the spirit of the evening, and when the music blared out, snake-charmer-like, I half expected a genie to appear. We danced an Egyptian conga, forming a long line that made its way round and round the rooms. While I laughed hysterically at Peter in his monastic white toga, he was having the time of his life.

Our next travel plans took us to Cairo, where we spent a few days, and then we headed home. I didn't particularly like the city, but it was interesting to see the Egyptian Antiquities Museum, which holds the world's most important collection of Egyptian antiquities. We saw the Great Pyramids, and just thinking about the effort it took to build them made the trip worthwhile. I never knew there were eighty pyramids in Egypt. We also saw the Sphinx, a lying-down lion with the head of a man, carved from natural rock.

Having spent over three weeks in ancient countries, it was a pleasant relief to return home. During the following years, Peter and I rented a car and drove through the Chateau country of France and ending up in the South of France for two weeks. The next year we flew to Athens, rented a car, and drove through the Peloponnesus. We ended up visiting Sicily and the cliff side village of Taoramina, then took the ferry off the island and drove to Pompeii. I was fascinated by Pompeii, imagining it as it was originally. We ended the trip in Rome and flew back to Phoenix. These trips were so much fun with Peter who was never angry, always upbeat, thoughtful, and loving.

The next year we visited Australia and New Zealand, which made for a long, long flight. We ended the trip with a cruise around Tahiti and various islands for a week. Recording memorable moments would not be complete without mentioning living through three days of a raging typhoon on Hamilton Island, which is part of the Australian Great Barrier Reef. Peter and I planned to snorkel in the beautiful blue waters only to awaken the first morning with winds blowing so violently the palm trees bent to the ground. We were in the middle of a huge storm with ominous black clouds and teeming rain. The waves crashed against the shore, and it was impossible to walk outdoors. No snorkeling that day, nor the next, nor the next. We watched a lot of movies and lingered over meals. The wind didn't subside until we were ready to leave. Having traveled so far, it was a big disappointment not to experience the Reef, but we were safe and ready to leave.

The flight back to Phoenix was endless, and we were both exhausted by the time we reached home. I was anxious to get back to work, and on the following day returned to the store to find business had slowed down considerably. After the incredibly busy eighties, designers weren't coming up with anything new and exciting, and the disastrous "grunge" look was all over the magazines. Everything was about jeans, torn, patched, cutoff, and messy, the more worn out the better. We decided to make some changes in our buy, doubling our sportswear budget and decreasing "serious" clothes like suits and dresses. Much of our evening wear shifted into evening separates. We limited our clunky shoe buy, necessary for our increased jeans inventory, and brought in more boots. Accessories were increased, as casual belts and handbags became important. I was constantly looking for something different to show with the new layered looks.

NINETEEN

First Things First

Family Reunion

In 1996 CAPRICCIO celebrated its twentieth birthday with a huge celebration at the Borgata. We took over the entire central courtyard, put the band out there, cleared an area for dancing, and placed tables and chairs for dining around the fountain. We asked all vendors to contribute something to the event, and we were elated with their generosity. We received over one hundred gifts, including a Judith Lieber handbag, a silk blouse, a hand-knit sweater, a beaded top, a wool shawl, and assorted other items that were all on display inside the store. Instead of raffling them off, we sold hundreds of balloons into which folded pieces of paper with the gifts written on them had been inserted. When the balloons were popped, out came the papers, and the person winning could claim her prize. It was a big hit, and between the balloons bursting, the squeals of joy, and the band playing there was pandemonium in the courtyard.

Inside the store we had a fortune teller and a caricaturist, and both were kept very busy during the evening. The main event, however, was our fashion show. We set up chairs and a runway inside the store and used ten beautiful models, ending the show with ten spectacular, sexy, beaded evening gowns flown in from New York especially for the occasion. The men, who didn't often see fashion shows, loved it and made a point of coming up to me afterwards to offer congratulations. We received outstanding press coverage for days. Cindy and Grant flew down from Colorado to make the event complete for me, but James decided not to fly down from San Francisco to join in the festivities.

I was disappointed, because the celebration of our success was also a tribute to me and our staff. It was a once-in-a-lifetime occasion, and I wanted him to be part of the experience. Instead, James stayed in San Francisco following his daily and evening routines, missing out once again on a major event at the store.

While we were planning the anniversary, I found myself reminiscing about those twenty years. How, in the early days, Bob Robb helped by giving us a substantial line of credit at his bank simply on a handshake. Limited for funds, we now had financial security with our vendors. Within six months we were able to repay the entire amount, a credit to the huge instant success of our store. We never, ever, needed to borrow again, thanks to long hours, hard work, and a great staff.

After five exciting years, we gave up our location in downtown Scottsdale in order to move into the Borgata, a jump from two thousand to ten thousand square feet. Already established as the best fashion store in town, we simply needed to add more of what we were doing and introduce something new to the mix. We decided to have an important shoe department and to bring in fine jewelry and furs as leased departments. We never dreamed how successful these would become.

For the first ten years, Gerry worked in the store and was responsible for all the financial parts of the operation. He interviewed and hired staff and did all general supervision. He was a charmer on the selling floor, and women loved his approval of something they were thinking of buying. As they swooshed past him modeling their latest temptations, he would comment, "Betty, that's the best looking outfit on you. You've got to have it." Or, "Thelma, that is certainly your color. Wear it to the club." Or, "Jan, that gown will be perfect with that gorgeous, new emerald necklace Bonnie just sold you. Take it home and show it to Bill. He'll love it."

In those days *OllieandGerry* was one word that stood for the perfect couple. Work together, play together, live together. It started falling apart when, in the early eighties, Gerry decided he wanted to go to Europe alone. He was drinking more and more and continually complaining about how many long years he had worked, and how much he deserved to retire. He gained quite a bit of weight, and his face was continually flushed. When he reached age sixty-five in 1985, he officially retired. He found nineteen-year-old Margaret Stone at this time, and suddenly he was on the bicycle exercising daily. With this first sign of motivation, the merry-go-round began.

From 1985 to 1989 we were separated, back together, separated, back together, separated, back together, and finally in 1989 we were divorced. Gerry moved to Oregon with his pregnant girlfriend, and as soon as the divorce was final they married. The marriage lasted about three years until Margaret finally left him and Gerry moved back to Scottsdale, alone.

What was happening to me emotionally when my marriage to Gerry fell apart? I spent weeks crying to myself. Having experienced the pain of infidelity and the agonizing nights alone during that first year of separation, I learned there is no way to go magically through the hurt except to go through it. In time I also discovered that the journey at the other end was a little easier. There was help waiting. I was taken by some inner force to an Alanon meeting that to this day I can't explain. At that first meeting I tried to share but couldn't stop crying. Everyone in the room had something helpful to contribute. I went to a second meeting, a third, a fourth. I just listened and cried. Finally, Bob, who later became a best friend, said to me in front of the entire group:

"Ollie, it's time you got out of the problem and into the solution."

Momentarily, I was hurt, but he was right. I was playing the victim role, poor-me-ing me to the hilt. I thought about it and decided I would attend ninety meetings in ninety days, a self-disciplining exercise. And I did. At the end, I decided to continue daily meetings, because I could see how it helped. When I first came to Alanon, I was lonely and hurt, angry and resentful, but through the program, I very slowly became calmer and more forgiving, willing to do what it took to achieve peace and serenity. Now, whenever

I'm sad or feel sorry for myself, I make out a gratitude list which immediately fills me with positive energy, calms me down, and makes me realize how much I have to be grateful for. It works every time.

Most people come to Alanon because they're living with the destructive effects of alcoholism—in my case, my father, two husbands, and now my son. Alcohol is very "cunning and baffling," and it triggers instantaneous changes in the drinker. One minute he's pleasant and the next minute he's screaming. These mood swings often escalate into huge fights, with the sober person ending up defeated and angry. I thought Alanon would teach me how to convince the alcoholic to stop drinking. Instead, I was told I was there for ME, that I needed help, that I needed to change. Not only was I powerless over my alcoholic, but I realized my life too had become unmanageable. My instant, screaming reactions to him bordered on insanity. What a shock to find I was about as sick as he was! It was reassuring, however, to learn I didn't cause my alcoholic to drink. I couldn't control it, nor could I cure it. But I could change ME.

And that's what I've been doing for the past twenty years, slowly sharing my experience, strength, and hope and listening to others share theirs. The more meetings I attend, the more recovery I experience. It just works that way. Each meeting is slightly different: some are step studies, others share problems. There are plenty of inspirational books to read, including my favorites, *Courage to Change* and *Paths to Recovery*. Along the way, you read sentences that stay with you: "*To love oneself is the beginning of a lifelong romance,*" or "*Each man's life represents a road towards himself.*" There are also some quick sayings that help in a moment of need: *One day at a time. Live and let live. First things first. Easy does it.*

First things first is one of the tenets of Alanon I frequently use. Daily. I pray to my Higher Power. I read spiritual literature, work with a sponsor, journal, and attend a minimum of five meetings a week. I learned that you can't hurry recovery, that all those years of living with an alcoholic diminished me, and that I had to work on myself in order to return to the strong, positive happy person I was before the beat, beat, beat of the emotional tom-toms took

My sister, Helen, with her husband, John

over. I think of it as my own private miracle, and I never forget that "Recovery is a process taken one day at a time."

It was at this time, the mid-nineties, that I went to my doctor for an annual checkup and learned that I had some pre-cancerous cells in my uterus. He recommended a complete hysterectomy as quickly as possible, but I asked if it could be delayed a week until I returned from a family reunion and burial service for my brother-in-law in Arlington Cemetery in Washington. He agreed and surgery was scheduled in one week. I couldn't miss this trip, because my sister, Helen, had been devastated by John's death. He had requested burial in Arlington, because he had been a Marine with battle experience.

Helen kept John's ashes in an urn at home and purposely delayed the burial for over seven months. They had been married almost fifty years, and she kept saying sadly, "I just can't give him up yet." She and I talked frequently during that period, and I was surprised to learn how John had taken care of everything, driving, check writing, income tax preparation. She was a professional nurse all her life, yet she was not a totally independent woman. She really leaned on him, and as a result, found herself "lost" and "needy" when he died.

It's been over eight years since then, and I see a totally different woman in my sister. She has gone through therapy, found a new church, and joined Alanon. Today she is strong and positive. We talk frequently, and we have formed a close bond we didn't have before. When she finally decided on the date for burial, we all knew she had come to accept his death and realized it was the future she should think about, not the past. I was immensely relieved that, at last, she came to that decision.

The night before John's services, we all met together for a reunion dinner. James had prepared a family film that he showed after dinner and later presented copies to the immediate family. He worked on this project for weeks, and I saw a side of James during this project that I hadn't seen in a long time. He concentrated on it intensely, and since I was in Phoenix and he in San Francisco, we talked on the phone several times a day. Sorting out the piles of old family pictures took forever, but we finally felt we had the right mix and arranged them all chronologically.

James called at this point, "Mom, I think you should fly up so we can finish this phase of the tape. I'd like to film the beginning with you introducing everybody and see how far along we can go. We can finalize our picture selection at the same time."

Visiting James was an ordeal because his condo was always a mess when I arrived. Every dish he owned was dirty and stacked up on the counters and sink. His bed linens looked as though they hadn't been laundered since my last trip. His computer room, where he spent most of his time, was in a perpetual state of chaos. There was hardly a space on the desk surfaces to use, or to find anything, or to sit down. The floor was filled with old newspapers, his mail (unopened), and things he simply threw down, using the entire area as a large wastebasket. You could hardly see the rug, so I had to tip-toe around or kick the debris out of my way. On the desk around his computer sat dirty dishes and glasses like so many tired old memories. I wondered how long they had been there, crusty with crumbs and dried up milk.

James was oblivious to all this, but I put my reaction on hold and started cleaning. I couldn't bear to cook in the kitchen, so I started there, completing three loads of dishwasher's time followed by cleaning the counters, floor, and stovetop. I asked James to clean the bathrooms and vacuum the floors.

"How can you live in this mess?" I asked woefully.

His answer was always the same. "You should see my friend's house if you think this is so bad."

There was dust everywhere. His dirty clothes were all over the chairs, couches, and floor. We picked up more than four loads, enough to keep the washing machine going all afternoon. James had laundered a big pile of clothes before my arrival and there it sat, one big lump, as a kind of I'll-pull-what-I-need-to-wear-today closet on the floor.

We worked all day and finished the major cleanup. For some crazy reason I had a giant-size dose of self-satisfaction. We ate a quick dinner and then started on the family film project. James took over and we finalized the selection. It was now ready for him to transfer on to tape. About ten o'clock he wanted to go to North Beach for his nightly socializing. I was exhausted and went to bed, and as I dozed off I repeated to myself, "Live and let live. Live and let live."

The following day and early evening James worked until he completed most of the project. We then did the beginning film with me commenting about each picture, from great grandparents to the present. James set up the lighting and rolled the film as I talked, covering every single person in the family. When we finally saw the finished product, I was very proud of the excellent job he did. I could hardly wait for the presentation in Washington, D.C.

Our family had never held a reunion before, so this would be the first time we would all be together. I had not seen my various nieces and nephews since they were little children, and I looked forward to getting re-acquainted. We all stayed at the Days Inn in Springfield, Virginia, just outside of Washington. The family consisted of my oldest sister, Anne, with her husband, Paul Panson. They had four children, Deborah Jean, Richard, Christine, and Linda, with three grandchildren among them. My sister, Helen, married John Pasternak. They also had four children, Nancy, Patricia, Geraldine, and Theodore with six grandchildren among them. I, Olga, divorced came with my daughter, Cindy, and my son, James. I have no grandchildren, and it looks like I never will. Cindy is unable to have children, and James doesn't want any.

There were about thirty of us at the reunion. We all had a chance to reminisce and find out what was happening to all our relatives. I had forgotten some of their names over the years, but everyone was open and friendly. Best of all, the family tape was a big hit, and James received all the well-deserved applause.

The following day, services for John were held at Arlington Cemetery. It was really impressive and moving. We were assigned an area for seating all our own and watched the Marine Band in full dress as they marched across the lawn and stopped in front of us while playing a rousing march. Four Marines conducted the folding of the flag ceremony, and one Marine carried it gently to my sister when they were finished. He spoke a few words to Helen, turned around, and walked away. It was a balmy July day, which helped set the mood, but when the bugler started to play "Taps," both Helen and I burst into tears. She clutched my hand tightly and as we looked at each other, I could see her sad face of resignation.

"I've done what John asked me to do. I've brought his ashes to Arlington Cemetery," Helen whispered. "I know he'll be happy now."

The band assembled once again and marched off. It was stirring music, a sad occasion, and an honorable tribute to a brave marine.

During those three days in Washington, I was worried about my upcoming surgery, and I was relieved to return to Phoenix after the reunion. A few days later I went in for the operation. When I awakened my first drowsy question to the doctor was, "Did you find any cancer?" I was terrified. "No, Ollie, we found no cancer." That was the best news of all and relieved my mind of all the imaginary scenes I had been obsessing over. I was in the hospital for three days, hurting with every move, until the doctor approved my going home to recuperate. I stayed in bed for two weeks, healing slowly until I felt strong enough to return to work.

A year later, in 1998, Peter went in for his annual examination at the Mayo Clinic, and his doctor discovered he had prostate cancer, a very aggressive kind of cancer. He recommended surgery as soon as possible, so within a week he was in the hospital. Dr. Ferigni was a specialist in this field, so Peter felt comfortable with his decision. After surgery he was in the hospital for three days and recuperated at home with a confident attitude. The doctor told him he would live many more years with the medications now available.

The reality of CANCER in his body started a whole new mind-game for Peter. As time went on he imagined various aches and pains as cancer-related. He visited the doctor regularly and was given luperin shots to help fight the cancer. For five years he did this and everything was fine. This last visit his PSA count went up, indicating the cancer had spread. The doctor gave him a luperin shot and, other than regular hot-flashes, his health has been pretty normal. His next trip will indicate whether his PSA has gone up or down.

TWENTY

Goodbye, CAPRICCIO

My Broken Heart

Peter and I were still living in Phoenix when, out of nowhere, I received a surprise phone call from Dr. Krant's real estate agent offering to buy our La Jolla store building. Dr. Krant's present building was across the back alley from CAPRICCIO, and he planned to expand his facilities by opening a spa in our building. He offered a price I couldn't refuse, so I decided to sell the building and close the store. It was a difficult decision, because CAPRICCIO had been in business for twenty-two years in La Jolla. It helped our summer volume, because it was peak season in California and the slowest months in Scottsdale. In addition, the apartment above the store was used as a second home by us. We entertained constantly, from beach parties at Windandsea to dinners for eight in the formal dining room in the apartment.

Once I decided to sell the La Jolla building, only the Borgata store in Scottsdale was left.

Our lease was up for renewal in 2000, and with management raising the rent beyond reason, I decided not to renew. It wasn't a quick nor an easy decision. We had been in business for twenty-four years and I still loved it, but I decided to retire in 2000 and move to California. I spent months looking up and down the coast for a new home, from Orange County to San Diego. Finally, I returned to La Jolla, a place I had grown to love, and nothing else I had seen could touch it. We have everything here—good weather, the ocean and beaches, theatre, opera, the university, Encanto Park, and the Zoo. We also have the airport nearby and any number of beautiful hotels, especially La Valencia right in the middle of town.

After searching in La Jolla for a home and finding nothing, my real estate agent, Linda Daniels, brought me to Crystal Bay. I had never been there before, but she said houses seldom came up for sale because it was such a desirable area. The home she showed me was on a lower level of Mt. Soledad and not what I wanted. Linda then mentioned another house would be available within a few weeks and promised she would contact me when it could be shown. Luckily, we were the first buyers to express interest in it, because it hadn't been listed yet. She arranged for me to see it before I returned to Phoenix, and the moment I walked in I knew this was home.

"I'll take it," I said. "What are they asking for it?"

After some negotiating, we agreed on a price and without hesitating I bought it. We closed on August 28, 1998, just two months before we sold our CAPRICCIO building in La Jolla. We were able to move all my furniture out of the apartment directly into the new home. What was left went back to the Scottsdale store. It was far simpler than storage, and we were able to start working on renovations of the new home immediately.

Peter was a big help at this time, packing boxes and sorting out small things to drive up to the house. He must have made twenty-five tedious trips, back and forth, usually with breakable objects requiring careful handling. He used my car and other than a routine, "I'm exhausted," now and then, pitched in without complaining too much.

I was busy with the movers at the building, separating items going to Phoenix from those going up to the new house in La Jolla. Among the pieces going to Phoenix was a huge ballroom mirror purchased in Paris. It was at least seven feet by nine, and the logistics involved in removing that from the building and down to the driveway were tricky. The frame was laden with hand-carved cherubs and was extremely heavy. Finally, six moving men figured a way out by easing the mirror on rollers and pushing it slowly out on the inner courtyard. With heavy ropes they lifted the mirror up, up, and over the rooftop and down to the driveway in a pulley-like arrangement. We held our breaths as it was lifted higher and higher with a swaying motion from the gentle afternoon breeze that caused the ropes to loosen. Fortunately, the mirror landed gently on the driveway, with a team of men holding it in place as it settled down.

Once the move was completed and our 6919 La Jolla Boulevard building was empty, we turned the keys over to Dr. Krant. We could now concentrate on our new La Jolla home on Mt. Soledad, with its breathtaking view of the Pacific Ocean. I took endless measurements to make sure my very tall antiques would fit. Other than one very large piece, they all did. To make that one fit our carpenter cleverly cut open a small corner of the ceiling and replastered it like before. Nobody has noticed it yet.

We made several major changes in the house. First we ripped up all the worn out wall-to-wall carpeting and installed 12x12, peachy-cream stone from Florence, Italy throughout the house. It transformed the interior. All the rooms had been painted a bland off white and desperately needed color. We hired a team of highly recommended painters, who arrived at eight each morning for weeks and promptly started work as a group, custom-coloring our walls with faux finishes and Venetian plaster.

We tiled two of the bathrooms with colorful Country Floors tiles, adding coordinated hand-painted sinks and counters that made them look very happy. When it came to the dreary kitchen, we decided to tear it out completely and replace it with a new Italian one in shiny lacquer red, designed by Pinin Farina, best known for his Ferrari automobile bodies. The cabinets were designed to undulate in soft curves and the drawers to silently slide out on rollers. We installed black granite counters and backsplashes and all stainless steel appliances. It was the kitchen of my dreams.

After these major changes were completed and all the furniture was placed, we began to feel at home. The only thing left was landscaping the front and back gardens, which had turned into neglected messes. We ended up removing everything in the beds, taking out mountains of dirt, and ordering endless quantities of rich soil to replace throughout. It was weeks before we could plant anything, and since we had no idea how much we needed to fill the space, it shocked us to see truck-loads of plants on a daily basis being brought in. The flower beds swallowed them up.

All the improvements transformed the house, and once it was completed I found, for the first time in my life, that I wasn't being pulled in any direction. This was the place I intended to stay. All the ups and downs I'd experienced were now memories able to be resurrected at a moment's notice, full of happiness one moment, sad and empty the next.

Looking back is a long trip.

One memory I will never forget occurred when Cindy was in her early thirties. She was obviously very upset, because her voice was trembling as though she were on the verge of tears. She had been seeing a therapist for over a year and finally had a break-through on some long forgotten experiences. She sounded very agitated by the memory of her trauma.

"I was eleven or twelve years old, Mom. I was sleeping in our house on East Georgia when I heard noises in the hallway that woke me up. The next thing I knew someone was in my bedroom pulling back my covers. I screamed, and the man put his hand over my mouth to quiet me." Cindy was sobbing.

"Don't be frightened. It's only me, your Dad, " he said in a muffled tone of voice.

"He smelled of stale liquor, and I knew he was drunk. He lifted my nightgown and the next thing he did was lay on top of me and start moving. He was breathing heavily, groaning and grunting, until finally, with one last gasp he was through. He warned me never to tell you, Mom."

"Oh, my God, Cindy, where was I when all this was happening.?" I was frantic.

"I'm not sure but I think you were on a buying trip to Europe. James and I always dreaded your leaving us on those long trips. We missed you so much."

"Did your Dad do this more than once?" I asked.

And as Cindy told me how frightened she was when she heard footsteps down the hallway, because she knew he was there, I was engulfed in such anguish I could hardly breathe.

She couldn't remember if he had done it again during the three weeks I was gone.

"You do believe me, don't you Mom?" She was hurting so much. I wanted to reach inside the telephone to hug and console her.

"Believe you? My dear, sweet Cindy, in your wildest dreams you couldn't lie about something so evil. How dare he do this to you in your own bed, in your own home, where you should always feel safe!" I was shaking with fury and disgust.

It happened almost twenty-five years ago, but suddenly I remembered how Cindy used to close her draperies tightly and shut the door to her room. She was in her early teens and never used to do that before. She insisted she heard noises in the hallway and was always afraid. She couldn't wait to go off to college and away from "that room."

When this all came to light, and she knew about her step-father's abuse, Cindy prayed and eventually confronted him. Of course he denied it and was furious she would accuse him of something so evil. In her perpetual state of goodness, she forgave him.

"I did it for me," she said quietly. "I needed to do it for me."

Every time I recall this horrendous reality, the same feelings return. My brain and my body fuse into a fireball of intense pain over the "act," but the perpetual guilt I feel because I was not there to protect her is even worse. My daughter, in her goodness, has found it possible to forgive him. I have not. Even though I have said the words, my heart is too heavy to mean them.

Maybe someday.

I realize my career had a way of claiming and devouring me all my life. It took me away from my children when they needed me most, and I rationalized to myself that I had to earn a living. It was true. But could I have done it any other way? I worked because I loved my work. That was the other half of the equation. When we opened CAPRICCIO in 1976, it was the beginning of a journey of self-fulfillment, but moving into the Borgata location in 1982 was the culmination. Buying our CAPRICCIO building in La Jolla in 1986 added to the work, but it was a wise decision. We could live above the store when we visited—particularly during the summer, when we stayed for two months.

Peter moved in with me in 1989, the beginning of the most kind and loving relationship of my life. I had been so used to alcoholic-husband abuse that his clean-and-sober personality was a welcome change. Peter stopped drinking when he was forty-nine, entered a treatment center in Wickenburg, Arizona, and then returned for a second go around until he "got it." Today he attends daily AA meetings and leads the life of an ideal recovering alcoholic.

He often talks about his two daughters and how much he regrets having missed so many years of their lives because of his drinking. He left the family when they were in their early teens. One attempt at reconciliation resulted in a flat, "no way." Life was no longer full of alcoholic behavior, mood swings, instant anger. Following his departure, both daughters' school grades went up, there was peace and harmony, and his wife did not want him back.

Today he has an on-going relationship with all three of them. His older daughter, Carol Luery, lives in Sacramento with her husband, daughter, and son. His younger daughter, Wendy Wilkinson, lives in Rancho Santa Fe with her husband, two sons, and daughter.

Peter's ex-wife lives near Wendy and we see her often at various parties at Wendy's.

Peter talks to his daughters frequently and always remarks how lucky he is to have this wonderful relationship with them. He goes to his grandchildren's soccer matches, horse shows, lacrosse games, graduations, and never-ending activities. It's nice being part of this family where I am welcome for all events.

Peter and I have been together for eighteen years now. Early in our relationship we did a lot of traveling. Between our travel-for-pleasure trips and my travel-for-business ones, I was getting burned out. It was necessary to be at the airport at least two hours in advance, and between the delays and unexpected weather conditions, we always considered our first and last days as "lost" time.